A WALK
WITH THE
RAINY SISTERS

OTHER BOOKS BY STEPHEN HUME

Signs Against an Empty Sky
And the House Sank Like a Ship in the Long Prairie Grass
Ghost Camps: Memory and Myth on Canada's Frontiers
Bush Telegraph: Discovering the Pacific Province
Off the Map: Western Travels on Roads Less Taken
Raincoast Chronicles #20: Lilies and Fireweed
A Stain Upon the Sea: West Coast Salmon Farming
Simon Fraser: In Search of Modern British Columbia

A WALK
WITH THE
RAINY SISTERS

In Praise of British Columbia's Places

Stephen Hume

HARBOUR PUBLISHING

Harbour Publishing Co. Ltd.
P.O. Box 219, Madeira Park, BC, V0N 2H0
www.harbourpublishing.com

Dust jacket photographs: Mixal Lake, BC by Suzanne Boyer; author photograph by Mark Van Manen for the *Vancouver Sun*; dragonfly by iStockphoto; ferns by Teresa Karbashewski
Dust jacket design by Teresa Karbashewski
Edited by Susan Mayse
Printed on 100% post-consumer fibre paper using soy-based ink
Printed and bound in Canada

Harbour Publishing acknowledges financial support from the Government of Canada through the Canada Book Fund and the Canada Council for the Arts, and from the Province of British Columbia through the BC Arts Council and the Book Publishing Tax Credit.

Library and Archives Canada Cataloguing in Publication

Hume, Stephen, 1947–
    A walk with the rainy sisters : in praise of British Columbia's places / Stephen Hume.

ISBN 978-1-55017-505-9

    1. Hume, Stephen, 1947– —Anecdotes. 2. British Columbia—Anecdotes. I. Title.

FC3811.7.H84 2010   971.1'05   C2010-903899-1

For Susan and Annie, fellow travellers

Contents

The Gift

We spend so much of our lives on cruise control, sweeping along in the comfortable bubble of our assumptions. What lies beyond the next bend is for the most part invisible, yet we speed calmly toward our expectations, always confident that the bridge will be there instead of the abyss.

We assume we'll see our friends again, that wives and husbands and kids will come home as they always do. And so we indulge ourselves in the petty tyrannies of parenthood and marriage, the nagging and squabbling over trivia, the evaded visits, the family bickering and the occasional grumpiness that comes of relationships we take for granted.

For me, the surliness emerged as exasperated barking at my three-year old after she waded into a puddle, swamped her new rubbers to the brims and filled the pockets of her fleece jacket with supplies for the "muddle pies" she planned to make for her stuffed mousie, Yay-tay.

A couple of days later, all forgiven and all forgotten, I took her off in great excitement to her play group. We live in the bush on an island with widely dispersed households, so the weekly meeting of the pre-kindergarten set is a big deal. Usually we meet in the community hall, the mums and I, the lone dad, stoke a blaze in the fireplace and swap gossip while the youngsters work out their territorial politics and at the same time get in some socializing.

This time, with a beautiful, crisp spring day interrupting the April showers, we were meeting instead at the marine park, a wild expanse of tangled woods, rocky outcrops and sandy beaches called Winter Cove.

Part of the strategy is to let the kids run themselves into the ground so that parents can look forward to early bedtimes and some respite from the high energy of childhood.

This time I was delegated to guide a party of three- and four-year-olds, led by Grady with his plastic sword and Derek with his homemade battle axe, in search of the dragon who lives under Boat Passage, a narrow gut between islands where the current boils and roars as the tides ebb and flood.

Off we went, stopping to examine every pile of dead branches, each winter-killed tree and a large, charred snag, all of which were absolute and unassailable evidence of the dragon's recent presence.

There's one thing about dragon hunting with preschoolers. The braggadocio may be loud, but nobody is bold enough to stray beyond arm's reach of the grown-ups.

An hour later, having edged wide-eyed past the narrows and scampered across the boardwalk through the swamp—Joe insists the murky water is home to the same crocodile that pulled the elephant's nose into a trunk—we emerged into bright sunlight, safely returned from our dangerous excursion.

The grassy meadow where the mums awaited us descends to a curved beach of white sand. Parents sat on the bleached drift logs and turned the kids loose with shovels and buckets.

As the tide fell, the kids followed it. I followed the kids, making sure they didn't stray from sight behind the decaying, rock-strewn remnants of an old landing.

My daughter, Heledd, and her pals, Lexy and Brianne, were collecting clamshells and filling and emptying their blue plastic bucket at the water's edge.

I turned to say something to the mums chatting on the drift logs, and when I turned back to check on the kids again, my daughter had vanished. Then a tiny hand clutching a blue bucket emerged from a swirl on the surface and went back under.

I never covered forty yards so fast in my best years of playing football.

Chest deep, I retrieved my child from the water where she was drowning. Had I not seen the bucket and the swirl, I'd never have found her under the waving canopy of bottom weed.

As it was, I fished her out, held her up by her ankles while she coughed and spluttered and carried her back to the beach. There, white-faced and wrapped in a dry sweater, she proved none the worse for wear. But the difference between a little girl frightened and one drowned had been a matter of seconds and inexplicable good luck.

It wasn't until many hours later that I sat bolt upright in bed, frightened into sleeplessness at the intensity of the reminder of what sinister peril may lie behind each sunny day.

We can't—and shouldn't—live our lives in constant fear of the worst that can happen. But we should switch off the cruise control and live each day as though the ones we most love will not be with us for another.

It rained again yesterday, a hard, sudden spring downpour at the fringes of a thunderstorm slashing northwestward out of Puget Sound. My daughter watched the lightning dance and dazzle around Mount Baker, and then, with a rainbow arching up from the white-laced reef offshore as abruptly as the rain squall passed, we went outside into the pungent air.

Heledd went to her favourite puddle. She wallowed in it. I kneeled down with her. We made muddle pies, got wet and dirty, and my heart filled with joy at the gift of it.

The Simple Joy of Rain

I'm not a guy who faithfully scans newspaper travel sections for winter getaway deals. I don't line up at the airports for a break in Hawaii or Fiji or Palm Springs or some Mexican beach in the Baja and then return with tales of iguanas, golf and too many green swizzles.

Nor am I that guy's gloomy alter ego, hunkered down and complaining about the dark, dank, insufferable months of January and February on the soggy, dreary, dismal West Coast.

What's to complain about?

A little damp is the price I pay for living amid the wonders of North America's temperate rain coast.

All things considered, it's a small price compared to what I fork over to the government to pay for wars in Afghanistan, a retractable roof for Vancouver's football stadium, temporary digs for speed skaters or the latest city hall facelift.

Complaining about winter rains on the West Coast makes as much sense as complaining that the sun rises too early in the morning. Things are what they are. This is a marine climate. It rains.

As for me, I love rain. I love it even when it saturates the slope we're on and we get a surfeit of it seeping into our deepest sub-basement, as it does every so often when downpours escalate to monsoons.

I love the subtle gradations of grey and the filtered light and the ever-changing sky. I love the gossamer drift of fine drizzle and halos around street lights and wraiths of water vapour drifting over depths in which the luminous globes of jellyfish pulse. I love the faint scent of the tropics that sometimes arrives with the Pineapple Express.

I love a shower's dimpling hiss across the still, glassy surface of a woodland bog and the drumming of raindrops on elephant-sized leaves of skunk cabbage. I love the splash and clatter of coho in a seething fall freshet to announce winter's imminent arrival and the massed trilling as the March rains bring out spring peepers to sing winter away.

My own winter mornings are always a surprise. Bands of fog layering the horizon in patterns that are never the same from one dawn to the next, with snow-clad mountains rising out of the sea in their capes of frozen rain: now hidden, now peeping out of the mist, now shining in a ray of sunlight, now draped in streamers of cloud.

What can be more of a feast for the eye than the reflections of clouds racing across the sides of tall buildings after a quick, sharp rain and a sudden blow from the sea, or the gleam of lights reflected from rain-slicked pavement so black it looks like you are about to fall into the abyss?

Who is immune to the sight of a small child in a yellow slicker and red gumboots jumping into the endless, joyous wonder of new puddles or to the hiss of a squall across the surface of Lost Lagoon, rising to rattle against your rain-coat, preferably one of those stiff, green Irish poacher's coats of waxed cotton?

At night I can think of nothing more satisfying than the staccato spatter of raindrops driven by a brisk southeaster while I lie snug in my bed, listening to my wife's steady breathing, and behind it, to the wind sighing through cedars in ancient voices from our dreamtime that speaks to all of us in the same language, a language everyone understands regardless of the self-imposed illusions of racial, ethnic, linguistic, national, religious or any other difference.

The sound of rain is the sound of life. The touch of rain is the quickening of existence. I love it.

A Little Madness in the Spring

Officially at least, winter's almost done. According to our fussy celestial accountants, in three short weeks the West Coast moves from deficit to surplus in the daylight department. At each solar noon during the subsequent astronomical quarter, the Sun will appear to rise a few degrees higher above the horizon until it reaches its zenith at midsummer.

This year, the seasonal books balance at exactly 5:48 a.m. on March 20, 2008, the vernal equinox. The first nanosecond after that, our days are longer than our nights. From that moment, our days will swell blissfully until they reach their solar maximum at summer solstice in far-off June, when they will begin to dwindle again. But let's not think on shrinking days just yet. For now the days will soon be fattening into glorious spring.

The accounting machinery of the heavens is extraordinarily precise. At the Royal Observatory at Greenwich, England, home by international decree of the Prime Meridian—starting point at the stroke of midnight for each new day, year, decade, century and millennium—austere mathematical tables set out the moment that winter deficit slips into spring surplus. For example, the year after this one, it happens at 11:44 a.m. sharp, and in 2010, it occurs at 5:32 p.m., and so on, ad infinitum.

Perhaps this cold, mechanical approach to calculating the arrival of spring is understandable, given the fact that selection of Greenwich as the Prime Meridian was the work of a committee of international bureaucrats. Forty-one of them from twenty-five nations decided on Greenwich in 1884 as a bloodless matter of the least inconvenience to the most. The United States had already chosen it as the reference point for its own time zones, and most of the world's shipping already used it for navigation, thanks to its adoption by the then ubiquitous Royal Navy.

At the conference, it's worth noting, France abstained from the final vote, although its proxy, the French colony of Algeria, moved that Greenwich Mean Time—on which seasonal calculations are based—be expressed as "Paris Mean Time diminished by 9 mins 21 secs."

Yet those of us who actually enjoy lives outside the inside of our heads—and beyond the office too—know that spring is anything but precise. It is messy, sexy, seductive, and where the snow is late leaving, often exceedingly sloppy. It some places it arrives in a dishevelled rush; in others it promenades down the boulevard blossom by blossom. It shows up in different places in different months, and nowhere on earth is its arrival quite so disorganized as here. British Columbia has a rumpled vertical landscape, compressed biogeoclimatic zones and a reach that extends from the semi-arid Mediterranean climate of the Gulf Islands to the temperate rain forests of Haida Gwaii to the alpine tundra of the Rocky Mountains to the continental climate of the Great Plains in the northeast.

Spring, for example, is already well entrenched in some parts of our vast and sprawling province of superlatives—highest and lowest, wettest and driest, most snow and least snow, etc. For more than a month, gardeners on the south end of Vancouver Island have been chortling about the February bumper crop of snowdrops and crocuses in their gardens and sending snide emails to less fortunate relatives groaning among the drifts at Icy Lake, Ontario, or braving the wind chill in Hairy Hill, Alberta.

But folks living in BC's high mountain country, on the Northern Interior plateau or east of the Rocky Mountains, in fact, just about anywhere outside the temperate climatic bubble that encloses the Lower Mainland and southeast Vancouver Island like a life-support dome, are still waiting for their spring.

They know that whatever the seasonal bookkeepers in Greenwich—or Paris diminished by 9 mins 21 secs if you're a Francophile—may say, the real spring, the poet's "spring, full of sweet days and roses," will arrive when and where it chooses and not necessarily on March 20.

Still, everyone can hope it will be sooner rather than later: dreaming bears, salmon hatchlings, rural farmers waiting restlessly for fields to dry enough for tilling, urban gardeners itching to get their hands off the computer keyboard and into the fragrant, loamy soil where they belong.

Soon enough winter will loosen its grip everywhere, and everywhere there is a taught sense of something about to happen, everything coiled for a sudden release, from the rising sap in the Pacific maples to the salmon emerging from dark gravel to begin their lifelong migration to the ocean deeps and back.

In the high country, the snow cornices will melt away, and the waterfalls cast in ice will melt and move again. In the valley bottoms, the trees will be full of songbirds again. The native Indian plums will adorn still-grey woods with their lovely, creamy blooms. The wetlands will thrum with the seductions of spring peepers, and the skies will echo with migrating waterfowl. The grey whales will arrive in their annual 22,000-kilometre journey up the West Coast. Closer inshore, silvery hordes of herring already dart in stunning synchronicity through their spawning shallows, accompanied by a host of sea lions, seals, eagles and diving birds.

Most striking among spring's signals of renewal and rebirth must be the early bloomers of the wildflower tribe, some humble, some gaudy. Among the humbler specimens to be found on a country walk are the catkins on the red alder, soon to be outshone by the luminous white petals of the Pacific dogwood.

The gleam of little snowdrops and the blue, yellow and purple glints of crocuses have been heralding spring since February in some places. On their heels will come narcissuses and early rhododendrons, from exotic cultivars to hardy drifts of the native mountain shrub. Then will come delicate chocolate lily, fawn lily, Easter lily, and in domestic gardens, the first daffodils and tulips.

Then the upland meadows and rocky outcrops, the urban window boxes, balcony planters and great botanical gardens will all erupt into that brief, brilliant palette of fairy bells and buttercups, shooting stars and salmonberry, red currant and foamflower, petunias and dahlias.

As the frogs sing their amorous symphony and the song-birds chirp and warble in their courtship dance, college and university students about to graduate will start to mysteriously pair off, and the rest of us will flood outdoors to be reminded again that the truth of the world and its wonders lie beyond numbers and dates.

To really experience the arrival of spring, one must go and search for it among the winter debris. It takes the form of pungent skunk cabbage unfurling in a blaze of yellow across muddy hollows, and the tiny fists of delicate buds preparing to unclench into the whispering of vivid green leaves at the first excuse of a warm day.

A walk in the woods at this time of year is an encounter with life in all its glossy resurgence, a reassurance that our lives are sweet, whatever stormy weather comes our way.

And if, here and there, spring fever breaks out a little early with the odd afternoon stolen from the boss, lunch eaten on a park bench instead of in the cafeteria, or class convening on the grass under a tree instead of inside a class-room, who's to care? For as Emily Dickinson once pointed out:

A little Madness in the Spring
Is wholesome even for the King.

The Song of the Mason Bee

I found Carla Pederson transplanting a luscious water lily from the black ooze at the bottom of a pond fringed with bulrushes out behind her home in the rural Comox Valley. Those big dragonflies they call darning needles swooped and darted overhead in iridescent splinters of green, crimson and blue.

She kicked off her gumboots and gave me a tour of Bees & Blooms, the tranquil Japanese-style garden that also serves as the nursery from which she sells unusual trees, shrubs and a host of annuals and perennials.

I say Japanese-style, because while her backyard garden-come-nursery has distinctly Asian elements, from the water features to the bonsai, it also displays qualities that are all Carla.

The heavily laden grape arbour and wine shed in one corner, for example, and the artistic arrangement of polished river stones. Or the display of old bottles retrieved by a neighbour from Cumberland, the pioneer coal mining town just up the road that's finding new life as a bedroom community with character amid the vinyl-clad, sprawling subdivisions.

But what I'd really come to see, I didn't notice until she pointed it out.

It was right behind my head, a plain block of wood hanging on the south-facing wall of the large garden shed that her husband Steve—he was away at his logging job on the northwest coast of Vancouver Island—had built for her.

Parallel rows of holes were bored in a rectangular grid, and the constant, buzzing stream of what appeared to be small black flies coming and going beside my head made me jump.

"Not flies!" She looked at me in feigned umbrage. Or maybe not so feigned, I thought. "Bees! Mason bees!"

Carla is an ardent evangelist for British Columbia's little native bees. Exactly how many species there are in BC— among the 3,500 that are native to North America and 800 that are native to Canada—isn't certain, although one recent count indentified thirty different species of wild bumblebee foraging in urban Vancouver.

Mason bees are actually common in Western Canada, which has 135 species of them. But they don't get the marquee billing of their better-known relatives, the domestic honeybees from whose hives flow golden torrents each year.

The mason bees are small and range in colour from drab black to iridescent blues and shimmering greens that reflect light with the same brilliant metallic sheen as the dragonflies. Unfortunately, Carla says, when they stray indoors, people often mistake them for houseflies as they try to bumble their way back outside against windowpanes, and they wind up getting swatted.

Carla thinks those of us who can't tell the difference be-tween a fly and a bee should smarten up and do something to educate ourselves. These solitary native bees are crucial-ly important in the process of pollination upon which the plant world—including our orchards, field crops and gar-dens—depends. For example, if you've noticed a decline in fruit production from your backyard fruit trees, it's less likely that your green thumb has suddenly turned brown than that you're actually suffering from a decline in your local native bee population.

Science has since discovered just how significant these small native bees can be, particularly in the pollination of tree fruits and berry plantations.

Most of us, at least those of us as ignorant as me, give all the credit to the honeybees we see fumbling at the clo-ver, visiting flowerbeds or droning around the crabapple blossoms.

"A honeybee will pollinate three hundred plants in a day," Carla told me. "A mason bee will pollinate three thou-sand plants a day. You do the math." Indeed, and her argu-ment is confirmed by science. One recent study that tracked a single wild bumblebee through Vancouver gardens found it visited six thousand flowers in five hours.

What distinguishes the mason bee from the honeybee is not just appearance but lifestyle. While honeybees are hive creatures and collectively produce honey in quantities that supports a large commercial industry, the mason bee lives alone, nesting and producing offspring by herself without the co-operation of other bees.

Carla uses a drill press to bore grids of precisely sized and spaced holes in blocks of wood that provide nesting tubes where the mason bees can lay their eggs, leave a honey supply and then seal off the chamber with a tiny wall of mud. This building habit earned them their name of mason bees.

So Carla doesn't just sell plants, she also sells housing intended to encourage backyard colonies of these busy little pollinators—they don't sting, by the way, and they are fun to watch—which help gardens thrive in both country and city.

Archeology in a Kitchen Garden

I woke this morning to forsythia crowned with rich yellow bloom and a blackened beam disintegrating into the herb garden.

This tiny plot behind a house built when Sir John A. Macdonald was prime minister has been kept outside the kitchen door since the days before supermarkets and freeze-drying. Garlic, chives, sweet basil, mint, oregano, sage, lemon balm and summer savoury mean the sauce in this house isn't seasoned from the shelf.

The herb garden is a living connection with an unwritten part of our long-vanished past. In the present tense, however, I am sweating to replace rotted mine railway timbers.

After almost a century, the timbers sag ominously. Behind their galloping dry rot, pressure from the shored-up bank has crushed in to create a dangerous bulge. One tie decays, and the whole intricate puzzle begins to unlock. The ties reinforced this cutbank for generations. To pull and replace the square beams is to slice through time and the document-driven half-truths of historians.

Women complain, quite reasonably, that their contribution to human progress is largely absent from our written history.

When these timbers first went into place in the Vancouver Island mining camp called Cumberland, black-faced fathers, husbands and sons jumped down from the steam locomotive Queen Ann and tramped wearily into the Big Strike and the Great War and the history books. The women were there too, though we seldom read about them.

Today the kitchen garden is a chapter of the story often ignored by male academics who prop up our patriarchy's self-congratulatory version of the past.

And so I wonder about the unnamed women whose intelligence and strength sustained their families out of this garden through lockout, strike, disaster and mass death at the coal face.

Here the reading of history is a pleasant task. You may sit in the shade and drink iced tea on a hot day, breathing the perfume of cinquefoil and laurel, watching the early bees fumble at the rock heather, listening to froggy melodies from down in the flooded bottoms of Coal Creek as they trill above the ageless harmony of wind in the cedars.

Under the bottom tier of timbers, smooth round river pebbles are laid neatly on the red clay. Where are they from, and why?

There's a clue from the starbursts of white crystal in the water-polished green stone. This is Oyster River snowflake rock. Somebody loved the look of these pebbles enough to pack them back from their canyons over thirty-five kilometres of raw trails and wagon road.

I suspect they provided a decorative border for the first

kitchen garden, buried by progress long ago. I salvaged the pebbles to build a new retaining wall higher up the slope.

In one deep garden layer, the slender, fluted shin bones of many deer tell us that when wages were a dollar a day and families were large—it's said more than a hundred children passed through the house in the century or more it has stood—the bush, not Safeway, was the meat larder.

Shards of crockery are the ledger of changing social status. Coarse stoneware occupies the lower levels. Higher up are layers of rising expectation: some startling hand-painted fragments, bright with red and green petals, bone china, a piece of etched crystal.

There's a thick layer of ash—fallout from a fire in Chinatown? Or the great fire of 1938 that raced 120 kilometres from Sayward to Comox Lake?

At the fringes, other relics: a handmade brick, a section of Chinese millstone, a miner's boot, a steel boiler recycled as a cistern. And nestled in the dark earth I find a mystery, the sensual curves of some small blue opium bottles. What dreams did they conjure? And for whom?

The timbers tell their own story. They worked thirty years in their first life at No. 4 Mine. The pithead was just beyond the pioneering Black community that's still named Coontown on old maps from a crueller, less enlightened time.

Today the Cumberland Historical Society's cairn pays tribute to the kinder side of history. It honours contributions by people like miner, prospector and legendary woodsman John Brown.

Reading the official history, you might be forgiven for thinking this place was happily integrated instead of fiercely segregated. "Nigger" Brown, as a meaner era named him, was not a bland, sentimental figure but a fascinating, complex character who dug more gold out of his fancy house than from his placer claims.

Secretly we know that only by acknowledging the pain—both given and received—can we fully affirm our collective humanity. Taking ownership of the hurtful side of our past makes possible both atonement and redemption, the only real foundation for progress.

Yet it's a human failing to want to celebrate the sunny memories and bury the bleaker ones. So we gloss over Coontown and the graves of someone's son or father that we marked only "a Chinaman."

And all too easily we forget the nameless, strong women who gave birth in back bedrooms and kept large families going from our small kitchen garden, tasks thought trivial by historians but that return to vivid life with this spring turning of the soil.

The Preservation of the World

The day comes early out back of the outback, which I'm first to admit is not how the people of the outer Gulf Islands feel about their relationship with the rest of British Columbia, particularly those unfortunate enough to live "on the continent."

Gulf Islanders feel more like they inhabit the navel of the world, a centre of simplicity from which they contemplate the distant frenzy under the Big Smoke—their term for the rat race of growth, productivity, wealth and power that stretches from Vancouver to Seattle and beyond. "As if," wrote naturalist Edward Abbey of the urban arrogance that blooms throughout North America, "gigantism were an end in itself. As if a commendable rat were a rat twelve hands high at the shoulder—and still growing."

On Saturna, outermost of all Canada's Gulf Islands—"out" being calculated, in the perverse manner of islanders, from Vancouver Island, not from Vancouver and the mainland—life unfolds with a tranquility that greets you as a physical presence.

Climb off the ferry and walk up from the dock beneath the green arbour that is the main road, step through the curtain of self-perception, and you enter a time that most of us have mislaid somewhere.

On the far west of the island, around from Breezy Bay but not quite so far as Murder Point, I found Jim Campbell, a pensioner who comes in from his sheep farm by boat or gets home with "a walk down the mountain."

He's referring to Mt. Warburton Pike, one of the highest in the gulf; if you care to climb to the windy silence of its summit, it offers a view to inspire poets.

The long, mountainous scimitar that is Saturna thrusts southeast toward the American boundary and the San Juan Islands, where a dispute over a stray Hudson's Bay Company pig wound up costing Canada half the archipelago. These had to be the most expensive spareribs in history.

This morning, rising with the first sliver of light over the distant American mountains, I find not a pig but a startled doe on the doorstep. She springs to the top of the steps in a single bound, and we both stand trembling, I in delight, the deer transfixed by the porch light.

To find this day's pig, I must pick my way carefully past puddles that glimmer along a muddy track curling into the gloom beneath towering cedars and the pale shapes of gold-clad maples.

The official pig cookers are up by starlight to slow roast what won't be consumed for another twelve hours. Beside the road, over the glowing coals of a hot alder fire, the carcass is dressed, split and trussed for the annual Saturna Island Pig Barbecue.

This is not to be confused with the world famous

Saturna Island Lamb Barbecue, a gussied-up party for off-islanders that draws 1,400 yachtsmen, yuppies and flesh-pressing politicians. The pig roast is for on-island folks and goes to raise money for the island's fire truck.

For all the summer cottagers and weekend islanders, not more than a few hundred people actually live on Saturna. They own the volunteer fire department, the community hall and the cemetery. There's no public debt to speak of.

By six o'clock in the evening on the night of my pig roast, at least two hundred islanders are packed into the old hall below the hand-lettered words of the national anthem. Sweatshirts mingle with slinky silk dresses; tables are crowded with writers and ex-writers, stray trollermen, loggers, liars and bellwethers. Feuding members of the Old Age Pensioners Association bury the hatchet for the evening for the good of the community.

Beer arrives unexpectedly at your table with a laconic, "You looked kinda thirsty, bud."

Meal service is by assembly line. Teenagers dish up the Spanish rice, younger kids hand out buns, and the littlest gravely offers pats of butter. Farther on, the pig is miraculously transformed. In an hour it's a heap of bones, and the dancing starts.

Much later, long after the dads have begun to slip away with armloads of sleepy kids, leaving mums to kick up their heels, I slide out for some fresh air and intrude on a grey-haired couple dancing among the coats. I pause as they swirl through the cloakroom and out to the rain-slicked street, a pair of old, old lovers.

The stars are bright in a clearing sky, and the air sharp as the hunter's moon. I stand in the shadows while they waltz slowly down to the government dock, then I slip down the timbered path for home. Music and laughter from the community hall dwindle until I hear only the sound of water droplets falling from high branches into the salal.

"In wildness is the preservation of the world," wrote Henry Thoreau. "I go to my woodland walks as the homesick return to their homes."

And islands, Henry. And islands.

Golden Islands of Serenity

The rocky, arbutus-studded outcrop known as Rum Island has the distinction of being closer to the United States than any other among Canada's western isles—which is why it was a secret depot for the long, black boats that ran bootleg booze across the border during Prohibition.

When I was in grade school almost fifty years ago, my teacher would drag our wandering attention back to English literature with stories about an earlier generation—his—that had earned its university tuition by smuggling.

They'd row across to the American side at night or in heavy fog, tying the contraband to Cuttyhunk halibut line and trailing it in their wake, where it could be cut loose if a patrol boat showed up—although few ever did out in that jungle of reefs, islets and tide rips.

And in more recent times—at least until the loonie went the direction of the peso—more than one bold islander has run a fourteen-foot tinny across to Friday Harbor on San Juan Island just before closing time, then loaded the boat to the gunwales with cheap drink for the Christmas party and conveniently forgotten about customs in the rush to get back. A few have been swamped on the way, their prized cases of rum and rye floating away as they frantically bail and try to restart the outboard.

Today the tawny five-hectare thumbnail where Rum Island juts into the turbulent waters at the confluence of Haro Strait and Prevost Pass—just over eight hundred metres west of the boundary that almost brought Britain and the US to war in 1859—is part of the new Gulf Islands National Park Reserve.

It's a peaceful place favoured by boaters for a sun-drenched family picnic among the constellations of magenta shooting star, purple satin flower and yellow cinquefoil.

In some ways Rum Island might symbolize the dream of the new national park that seeks to place these still-pristine corners of creation under a protective umbrella. Not all the Gulf Islands are destined for the national park, and not all Gulf Islanders are enthusiasts. Who but the most selfish and wizened of spirit, though, won't welcome a park that will make it possible for all Canadians to experience the astonishing intersection of natural beauty and fascinating history that characterizes this magical archipelago of the southern Strait of Georgia?

North and west from here, the rest of the two hundred Gulf Islands scatter across the blue sea like jade and amber fragments spilled from the broken necklace of some ancient, forgotten goddess. They range from the bulk of a pastoral Saltspring Island now groaning under the gentrifying weight of newly transplanted Torontonians and Albertans to the near-naked and uninhabited Belle Chain Islets, where the *Kenkon Maru,* outbound for Vladivostok with a load of rolling stock for the Siberian railway, was wrecked in a snowstorm in 1916.

From laid-back Lasqueti to the former leper colony of D'Arcy, from Bowen the Vancouver bedroom community to De Courcy with its dark, scandalous history of Brother XII's religious cult, each island has its own mood, ecology and culture. Some are near-desert, with prickly pear and stonecrop; others have cathedrals of eight-hundred-year-old Douglas fir. Some are counterculture enclaves that hearken back to the days of Flower Power; some are yuppified fort-resses of imported NIMBYism. Pender Island commuters differ from Hornby stay-at-homes as much as Vancouver's West Enders differ from Surrey suburbanites.

Lying between the continent and the dry east slope of Vancouver Island, the tide-carved shelves of honey-col-oured sandstone that form the Gulf Islands' beaches have their origins in the Cretaceous period. Fossils from sixty-five million years ago—markers from the end of the age of dinosaurs—still surface in the weathering sedimentary shorelines.

Once these beaches were ancient seabeds. The warm waters above were populated by plesiosaurs, ichthyosaurs, gigantic sharks and ammonites. Now they tilt out of the sea on the upthrust of vast tectonic forces where the Juan de Fuca Plate buckles and slides under North America.

The southern Gulf Islands were attached to Vancouver Island until Ice Age glaciers carved them loose. They lie in the semi-arid rain shadow cast by the high mountain spine of Vancouver Island and by Washington state's Olympic

Peninsula, well-shielded from the hurricane-force winds that buffet the outer coast.

Sea lions, orcas, sharks and sailboats all cruise the gentle waters. Silvery hordes of salmon sweep past on their way to the Fraser River. Giant ling cod lay ambushes in the kelp forests.

If there's an ideal place to contemplate the marvels of this corner of the world and to understand why a new national park in the Salish Sea is long overdue, perhaps it's to be found here on Rum Island, a microcosm of the microcosm.

On a clear night when the annual February high pressure zone drives off the rain clouds, I can look to the habitation glow that arcs like a second Milky Way around the curved horizon from Victoria to Seattle to Vancouver. It wasn't there when the rum-runners plied their midnight trade.

It's then that I comprehend with startling clarity why these islands of serenity adrift in a moon-silvered sea, surrounded by an emerging megalopolis, are a national treasure that desperately needs formal protection from the tidal waves of population and the accompanying pressure for urban development that will challenge and transform them in the coming decades.

Doing the Rain Dance

I've always loved a good electrical storm. Once I even climbed to the roof of a forty-storey prairie highrise to watch the lightning bolts lance into the surrounding countryside. So I happily rose in the pre-dawn hours to catch one of nature's sultry light shows sizzling over the Strait of Georgia.

These shows are free, wherever you happen to be, and if the musical score is limited to percussion, the special effects more than make up for the absence of Andrew Lloyd Webber.

I got a hint that something was on the way earlier in the evening. Skies were clear, but a glossy, ominous swell began sucking up and down the sandstone ledges that step down from our house on the north shore of Saturna Island. It gurgled up to chase me out of the slippery tide pools where I'd been scrounging for limpets and little blue mussels for flounder bait.

My four-year-old had laboured all afternoon to assemble her flatfish jig from an old coat hanger, one of my redundant trolling weights and some fish hooks she chose at the general store—where the groceries trail off into hardware—as much for their pretty Norwegian curves as for their effectiveness.

She insisted on the rig recommended by her late grandfather, a wily old bucktailer who never turned up his nose at a nice mess of sand dabs.

I handled the split rings, swivels and pliers. She gave specific directions.

But then I thought about the swell and getting her ashore from my little aluminum skiff if it got any heavier. To cries of betrayal, I put the promised rock sole expedition on hold.

Instead we went down to visit our local endangered species preserve—East Point Lighthouse—where we sat on the rocks and watched the shipping lanes in Rosario Channel.

We like to watch passing ships and guess at the cargo—crude oil for Cherry Point refinery in Washington, new cars for the Richmond auto mall, grain for China, lumber for Japan where Heledd's cousin Chris is going to school this year.

One huge, boxy, red-sided bulk carrier throbbed into view. It looked less like a ship than a floating warehouse. I asked Heledd what it was carrying. She answered without hesitation, "That's the U ship, Dad. It's full of Us."

And where might it be going with all these Us?

"To the word store in Vancouver. That's where people who make books go to buy all their words. You have to have a lot of Us to make enough words for everyone."

We didn't wait around for the Y ship because the lights

on Grouse Mountain were already forming one on the mountainside, a glittering signal that dusk was falling fast.

Just before bedtime, with the bats flitting among the trees to hunt for insects, we hiked up the hill to take one more anxious look at our water levels. Two five-thousand-litre tanks store the precious community supply gleaned from a well that doesn't put out much even in the rainy season. They were down to a scant seven hundred litres, not much for the twelve households on the system. Of course, we consider ourselves lucky—some of the folks out on East Point are trucking in their water.

It's been a thirsty summer here. Barely a trace of July rain recorded up at the Environment Canada meteorological station, and now the hot, dry month of August stretches dustily ahead.

People call this the Wet Coast, but here in the semi-arid outer Gulf Islands, where you can sit on a cactus patch if you're not careful, water is far more likely to be a topic of spicy conversation over beers and barbecue than sex, religion or politics.

Whose grass is brown and for how long? Who has selflessly given up watering the geraniums? Who bathed from the rain barrel this morning? Who came from Vancouver for the weekend and indulged in a long, leisurely shower together that means nobody else can do laundry for a week? Who smugly confesses to installing super-low-flow toilets? Who, to achieve the zenith of one-upmanship, eschews the flush toilet altogether and retreats to the privy in the woods to conserve water in the drought days?

Water, that commodity we all take for granted so much of the time, has been of particular concern for me lately, and not just as one of those householders who doesn't relish the idea of being reduced to swims in the ice-cold saltchuck to get clean.

I suppose that's the real reason I was up in the small hours watching the storm. I was praying for a soak to shut up those big-city talk show hosts with their brainless chatter about fun in the sun.

At least I got to enjoy my own private Symphony of Fire. Dazzling sheets of light flashed through layers of cloud that pressed down on dark mountains. Far below, the sea was sleek and restless, full of subdued glints. It reflected the lightning across the mother-of-pearl undersides of glowering, midnight black thunderheads.

There was not a spot of rain. This was troubling. In my secret political life, I'm one of the three trustees for Saturna Shores Water District. It's not an office you run for. Like the Black Spot, you get handed the job when your neighbours turn on you.

Conservationists all, we've raised the water rates by 100 percent in two years. So if the fitful well now dwindles to a brackish trickle, I'm the one the ratepayers have every right to ask, "What are you going to do about it?"

I don't know. A rain dance?

Sexy, Sultry, Star-struck Summer

Blue skies and heat shimmers indiscriminately grace shopping mall parking lots, sandy beaches and mountain rock faces, leaving no doubt that summer has arrived, although just when this season of burnished opulence began is always a matter of argument.

Roderick Haig-Brown, Canada's poet laureate of the outdoors, said he'd take any warm, sunny day in June, perhaps even late May.

"And I am just as willing to talk about spring run-off when the snow melt comes pouring down the hills through late June and on into July. Seasons are quite flexible things really and it's not very profitable to try and tie them down to dates."

But at the Dominion Astrophysical Observatory on Little Saanich Mountain, the first day of summer is specific. It is the precise moment at which the apparent track of the Sun arrives at a point 23 degrees and 27 minutes north of the equator.

Our planet is tilted about 23.5 degrees from vertical. At

this point in its orbit, the tilt leans toward the Sun and into the 130 trillion horsepower of solar energy we receive every second. Summer begins when the light waves delivering this energy are directly overhead at the Tropic of Cancer. And the closer these rays come to vertical, the more heat they deliver to the northern hemisphere.

About 480 kilometres overhead, in a 400-kilometre-deep band of rarefied oxygen and nitrogen called the thermosphere, incoming solar radiation raises temperatures to almost two thousand degrees.

That we think forty degrees in Osoyoos is insufferably hot is a testament to the insulating power of the thin envelope of atmosphere we so consistently abuse.

There, in the vast heat exchange mechanisms involving air, land and ocean, the weather and climatic patterns that determine our seasons are born.

The unequal heating of the earth's surface, a product of the globe's curvature and axial tilt, is the engine driving the great vertical transfers of energy that modulate the Mediterranean-type climate that blesses the southwest coast and the temperate marine climates ranging from Vancouver Island to the Alaska Panhandle. In this temperature differential are created the prevailing winds that suck up water vapour, form clouds and carry life-giving rain to the land.

Dave Mackas, a leading plankton ecologist at the federal government's Institute of Ocean Sciences, studies these large mechanisms, so vast as to be invisible, and how they affect the tiniest organisms, equally invisible, and thus profoundly shape the season we call summer on the West Coast.

He watches how wind and water move off the outer

coast of Vancouver Island, combining to create conditions that cyclically inhibit and encourage plankton growth.

The Pacific, he points out, is a huge thermal reservoir, radiating warmth to the adjacent land in winter when the effects of the sun are diminished, absorbing it in summer when terrestrial British Columbia heats rapidly under near-vertical solar rays.

In winter, when the land is cooler than the sea, prevailing winds are drawn from the south, off the ocean. As they pass, they pick up water vapour, dumping it as rain and snow when they collide with steep coastal mountains. This is why four of North America's largest rivers rise in British Columbia.

On land the combination of precipitation and surplus heat from the summer sun triggers the explosion of growth that characterizes the rich biodiversity of BC's temperate coastal rain forests. Behind the mountains, the rain shadow intensifies in summer. The grass goes tawny and the forests are sparse.

Winter's prevailing winds push cold deep-ocean water toward the BC coast, where it sinks. This water, less rich in nutrients, suppresses the growth of marine micro-organisms, which is why our seas are so much clearer during the cold months.

But in summer, because the land heats much more rapidly, these patterns reverse. Outflow winds from the northeast tend to prevail. Often the rapid heating of the land creates stable high pressure zones that block any weak inflows from the ocean—the reason summer so often brings clear skies and hot days to the east side of Vancouver Island and the Interior.

Now the friction pushes surface water seaward, generating a nutrient-rich upwelling from the continental shelf. These upwellings create some of the world's most productive waters. Coupled with the intense sunlight of summer, they produce massive plankton blooms, some of them lethal, like the toxic red tides that sometimes close shellfish harvests up and down the coast.

Yet most plankton are beneficial. They begin a food chain that sustains an astonishing array of invertebrates, herring, juvenile salmon migrating from fresh water, pelagic predators like hake and tuna, countless seabirds and aquatic mammals. Seal, sea lions and toothed and baleen whales all congregate to reap the bounty. It's no accident that July is when the seals whelp and rocky foreshores ring with the bark of pups.

For most of us summer remains a time of subtle changes in sensation. It is when the vivid, unsullied palette of spring buds gives way to the denser, calmer green of mature foliage.

There's more to this than meets the eye. Just as the energy exchange is taking place offshore, another takes place on land. Our short but intense summer is the window in which plants convert abundant light to the energy they must store to produce new leaves in the lean days next spring.

In a landscape where seasonal variations are great, one of nature's ingenious adaptations to a temperate climate is to be seen on every hillside.

Our coniferous forests are not there by chance. Evergreens keep their leaves all year round, a strategy for trapping the energy even of the weak winter sun. So Stanley Park offers a lesson in natural selection. There the mature conifers are so efficient at capturing available light that the forest floor beneath appears gloomy on the brightest summer day.

Brightening the gloom are glints of colour. In the native languages of our north coast, this is the time of big berries. Indeed, even the stumps in urban landscapes are crowned with the bright red of huckleberries. The thimbleberries and the tiny white fruit of the arbutus have largely fallen, but our little native black caps glisten along road margins. Oregon grapes fatten among their glossy leaves and big Himalayan blackberries ripen where their brambles cascade over abandoned fences and vacant lots.

If summer brings the first hints of autumnal abundance, it heralds the same for large segments of our economy. Summer is big business, and not just for the shrewd entrepreneurs who exploit an aging Baby Boom's infatuation with receding youth.

Take the lowly gas barbecue. Sixty percent of Canadian households have one. This bit of summer equipment represents a collective capital investment of $876 million. Barbecue cookbooks routinely chalk up sales of 250,000 for a first run.

And as a summer status symbol, the gas barbecue turns out to be as over-engineered as the muscle car. Your average 45,000 BTU grill puts out enough energy to heat a suburban bungalow in January.

One of those Canadians born between 1946 and 1966 will turn fifty every seven seconds until the year 2016. But the Beach Boys generation is still urged to associate summer with wedge-shaped torsos sculpted by Michelangelo and breasts that defy gravity.

These are the months when the otherwise demure are encouraged to make frank public displays of their physical assets, which is why cellulite and flabby abs depose Communism as the enemy of life as we know it—at least in the marketers' cosmos.

Yet for all its association with youth, summer is really the sleek middle age of the calendar. It is that quarter in which the animal kingdom begins to pad itself with fat in preparation for the hungry months ahead. At midsummer everything stands at the zenith of its powers but has not quite realized the rewards.

The rewards sometimes seem distant.

Tar melts. A blue sheen of ozone glimmers over the megalopolis from Vancouver to Olympia. Freeways glitter with mirages. Commuters calculate how long the air conditioning can stay on recycle before the threat of oxygen starvation outweighs the risk of carbon monoxide poisoning. A reasonable worry: summer smog in the Fraser Valley costs British Columbians almost $10 million a year in lost crops and is thought responsible for thousands of respiratory fatalities. And research shows a measurable loss of IQ for every hour spent in traffic gridlock—ergo, summer, more than any other season, reminds us that the more we drive, the dumber we seem to get. This, perhaps, is why summer appears to be characterized by the desire to get as far from the street life of the automobile as that same automobile can carry us.

Transhumance seems an odd concept to apply to a city. But a summer-long migration to the country and back is what we practise. Despite fluctuations in travel by visitors from overseas and the US, British Columbians continue to account for two-thirds of the overnight non-business trips in BC. Almost half of this travel is during the summer and generates the majority of business for small hotels and motels.

Almost 90 percent of the province's inhabitants have used a provincial park at least once, and in an average year six of every ten British Columbians will visit a national or provincial park. In Vancouver alone the overnight person trips for summer leisure exceeds the total urban population by one-third. Swimming, hiking, water sports, cycling and birdwatching account for the majority of overnight trips by British Columbians.

One in five Canadians who overnight for leisure in the summer now goes camping. Small wonder, then, that provincial campgrounds installing a new telephone reservation system were overwhelmed on summer weekends. And hikers on the remote West Coast Trail leave in flights, like golfers at an overcrowded course.

Does this suggest too many parks? Or too few? Or that we should seriously rethink our whole approach to urban design?

Meanwhile, on suburban picnic grounds, the market rules. Tables that caught the first sun in early April and couldn't be had for love or money are now shunned. It's the shade that's in demand. Not surprising, since Environment Canada warns that the frying time for exposed flesh can be measured in minutes at this time of year—even with 40-SPF rated sunscreen.

Can it really be more than half a century since Jacques Heim shocked Paris with the itsy-bitsy, teeny-weeny bathing suit the world called the bikini? Who'd have guessed that the height of risqué style, designed to bring sweat to the upper lips of adolescent boys, would become an icon of folly in the age of ultraviolet? The *Medical Post* says bikinis may boost the risk of melanoma for young women.

Yet, even as we swelter homeward through the rush-hour crawl, all but the most preoccupied notice that these are the days when a languid grace descends from heaven.

Business gears down for the dog days as vacationers depart on the rigidly programmed schedule of summer holidays that was designed not for the post-industrial state and the home office of the twenty-first century but for the little red schoolhouse and the seasonal agrarian economy of the nineteenth.

Even the raucous, arid chatter of the internet seems strangely subdued. And in those areas not condemned to the perpetual green springtime of suburban lawn care—or the productive rigours of irrigation farming—the fields and hillsides of July and August are accompanied by a peculiar, scorched hush.

These are the months of consummation.

The spring bloom that flooded the landscape with perfume and colour, the throbbing sensuality of animal courtship, have all begun to ebb. The first great burst of pollination is now complete, the honey flow is underway and dazzling sexual display gives way to fruits and seed pods that swell on branch and vine.

"The force that through the green fuse drives the flower," Dylan Thomas called it. Deny as we might, it drives us too.

Among the phenomena for which there is now powerful statistical evidence of seasonality in human behaviour are levels of sex hormone secretion, sperm counts, the onset of menstruation and frequency of sexual intercourse.

Does the police blotter swell in summer? Researchers writing in the *Journal of Endocrinology and Metabolism* note that men's testosterone levels peak in July.

Do torrid days and velvet nights traditionally bring summer romance to the cosmology of teenagers awakening to their biological imperatives? Loss of virginity turns out to be another event that can be correlated to the season.

And birth records in North America, Europe and Japan show that conceptions peak in June and July. In South America, Australia and New Zealand, the peak months are December and January—confirming the seasonal nature of the pattern, for summer is reversed in the southern hemisphere.

Since sperm counts seem to reach their nadir in summer, does logic suggest that frequency of intercourse might be the factor that offsets a seasonal decline in male fertility?

Our intellects prefer to overlook such patterned connections to natural cycles. Yet scientific method suggests our behaviour often responds to unconscious yearnings fixed in our DNA.

Is it surprising, then, that high summer is when most young people decide that what they found in each other last spring must be love? Or that summer is the season of weddings? Or that many of us will carry to our graves the indelible memory of some youthful summer encounter under starry skies?

These subliminal messages from undomesticated nature speak to us clearly in languages we often pretend we can't hear and don't understand, although our bodies seem to get the message loud and clear.

But around us, the wild grasses have all headed out. Their nodding seed heads whisper on the light summer airs. High above on the broadleaf maple, dense clusters of seeds with their helicopter vanes begin to shed the odd whirring outrider. The vivid yellow on the broom gives way to black seed cases that sound like firecrackers as they spring open to broadcast their contents.

The sap that rose so furiously six short weeks ago has, in the words of Llewelyn Powys, suddenly conjured out of light and water and thin air a miracle—billions of new leaves that toss and rustle from horizon to horizon.

Amid all this, nature appears to hesitate. It is as though the countryside was resting while the earth pauses at aphelion, gathering itself for the next lap into darkness and winter.

In our endless elliptical journey through space, midsummer means we are now the farthest we will get from the Sun. Even as we savour it, the season for which we've all been waiting is imperceptibly ebbing away.

From now until just before Christmas, the celestial chronograph will shorten each day by two irrevocable minutes. Two minutes? What's that? The time it takes to light the gas barbecue.

By the beginning of August, the span between sunrise and sunset will sink below fifteen hours, not to be restored until the middle of next May. But for now it's enough that the days are long and the sunlight pours down like amber honey.

Around us the natural world seems imbued with tawny hues and all the infinite variations of gold. On the high peaks of the cordillera, the winter snow pack borrowed from the sea last winter sluices into the watersheds, stirring the Fraser into an immense brown plume that stains the Strait of Georgia.

All too soon the clockworks of heaven will shift the equilibrium at sea, as it always has. Scientists like Dave Mackas will note the light switch. The land will cool. Green leaves will acquire a brittle quality and the great migratory cycles will both end and begin anew. And most of us will look up from a balmy evening drink on the patio or deck and sense that one more summer is grown old and now recedes from us into that past whose richness we may always remember but can never relive.

The Secret Dance of Dragonflies

The pond has no name, and since it deserves its seclusion, I decline to provide directions. Yet this humble patch of boggy ground serves as a quiet reminder that unseen dimensions constantly intrude into our tame and ordered world.

On a sunny day like this one, with puffy, white clouds scudding overhead and the surrounding meadow grass dappled with fleeting shadows, the sounds of city life are lost in the rustle of the breeze through immense old broadleaf maples. Fringed by the primeval green of mare's tail and the darker hue of reeds and rushes, covered with water lilies just now bursting into bloom and floating strands of smartweed, the pond provides a brackish oasis of calm a scant hundred metres from busy city streets.

That tranquility is all illusion. Although the scale is tiny, there's little peace in this enclosed aquatic world. Take that drab-looking water bug with the segmented, armoured carapace. It could be from the movie *Alien*. The modest lower lip actually hides a hinged extensible jaw that lunges out to seize and devour prey. The water bug is a nymph—the aquatic larva—of a dragonfly, waiting to undergo its metamorphosis into one of the big electric blue darners that go skimming across the water in graceful hunting patrols.

To get to this hidden wonder bursting with life, I followed the Indiana Jones of bugs, Rob Cannings, the khaki-clad curator of entomology at the Royal BC Museum.

He belongs to BC's pre-eminent family of natural history. Brothers Richard (former curator of the Spencer Entomological Museum at the University of British Columbia) and Sydney (fifteen years as curator of UBC's Cowan Vertebrate Museum) co-wrote the award-winning *British Columbia: A Natural History* in 1997. Rob contributed the aquatic biology to their subsequent collaboration, *The World of Fresh Water*, in 1998.

In 2002 he published *Dragonflies of British Columbia and the Yukon*, a lovely handbook with 125 colour plates to show those consulting the text what they are looking at and detailed notes and diagrams explaining the behaviour and life cycle of BC's three families of the dramatic flying insect.

We met in the cramped twelfth-floor office Rob shares with twenty thousand specimens, each labelled and stored in a transparent envelope of the kind commonly used by stamp collectors. These envelopes transformed the public face of entomology. When I was a kid visiting the old provincial museum when it was a cramped, neoclassical stone annex of the provincial legislature buildings, each specimen was stuck on a pin, with row after row displayed in coffin-like wooden cabinets with glass tops. Now specimens go neatly into vertical steel filing cabinets on tracks, much like the filing system in a modern corporate library. The system is far more convenient for researchers, if not quite so mesmerising for youngsters.

"Just pop the whole envelope into a self-sealing Baggie, and you can mail your specimen to researchers around the world," Canning says. "And we can get many more specimens into much less space, which is always at a premium."

While I admire the new techniques that preserve many of the brilliant metallic tones of blue, green, crimson and yellow that make dragonflies such a colourful part of summer in BC—we have five hundred species—he tells me how his own appreciation for natural history evolved.

"I was born in Summerland and lived right above Trout Creek and later at Penticton. My dad was a real keen naturalist," he says. "Ponds attract kids, and I've always liked aquatic entomology. But only after I'd completed my MSc did I study dragonflies."

That was when he fell under the influence of Geoff Scudder, now professor emeritus of zoology at UBC and renowned for his passionate arguments for biodiversity and the fragile grasslands of the South Okanagan.

Back in 1977, Rob worked with Kathleen Stuart to prepare a little handbook on dragonflies for the provincial museum. He discovered the whole rich taxonomy of creatures with names like river jewelwings and rainpool gliders, pond damsels and sedge sprites, emerald spreadwings and blue dashers, saffron-winged meadowhawks and crimson-ringed whitefaces. I mention the unusual poetry in these names, and Canning chuckles.

"A bunch of us invented the common names because nobody would publish field guides if we used the Latin."

I can see his point. Western pondhawk does have more

of a ring to it than *Erythemis collocata*, unless you prefer Lucretius in the original.

In these names he found a twenty-five-year passion for the soaring, darting speed demons of the insect world. It led him to a global community of dragonfly researchers and his own life work of studying the diversity and geographic distribution of the species in BC.

"In Northern BC we found four new species to the province," he says. "The Quebec emerald lives in peat bogs. It's rare, even in the East. Lo and behold, we found it around McBride and all the way to Williams Lake. That was neat, to find something so rare and relatively unknown."

His enthusiasm is infectious. Dragonflies, he writes in his new book, have fascinated people down the ages with their colours and dashing flight. Poets have written about them, artists have painted them and children have marvelled.

"The hot thing right now is the incredible popularity they have in the general naturalist community," he says. "Ever since the 1960s people have been interested, and as the world gets more and more urbanized, people are more sensitive to what's being lost. People are really interested in their backyard pond. In a way, scientists like me are just trying to catch up to the public."

With that, we collected his specimen nets and set out for the secret pond he's been visiting for years in what's now called the urban-rural interface. We made our precarious way along the top of a steep bank that's protected by a link-steel fence, fending off brambles and picking our way through brush.

"I discovered the larvae of a rare specimen right here in

this pond, the orange-veined meadowhawk," he says as we pop out into the little meadow.

And then, with a deftness that belies the lack of binocular vision that's the legacy of a childhood accident, he snares dragonflies on the wing with such a delicate touch that not a single one is injured.

Carefully he extracts them from the mesh so I can examine the huge, domed eyes with thousands of lenses, trying to imagine seeing the world in 360 degrees. Massive external shoulder muscles can move gossamer wings so swiftly they can fly at up to sixty kilometres an hour. He even perches one on a finger so I can feel the Velcro-like hooks that enable them to catch and eat their prey on the wing.

In a way, it's like a window into the most ancient past. The ancestors of these insects stalked the swamps of the Carboniferous—more than three hundred million years ago—on wings that spanned almost a metre. Their successful descendants retain many of their features.

Perhaps it's that span of time that lends urgency to Rob's studies of distribution and habitat for these amazing creatures.

"I'm convinced that climate is changing," he says. "It's a big issue and it's going to make a big difference to this province. Who knows what happens to Northern BC when climate changes and water becomes scarce? We are trying to get a really detailed picture of where these dragonflies range, over the seasons as well as over the landscape."

It's not just climate that offers threats. From Burns Bog in the Fraser River Delta to the Codd Island Wetlands near Pitt Meadows, there are fights on all across the province to save the dwindling wetlands of BC from human exploitation and destruction.

In the meantime, the lost world of this secret little pond dreams on through languid summer days while dragonflies dance across its surface like brilliant splinters of nature's prism, messengers from the distant past sent to remind us of everything that is ours to lose.

Of Cuban Coffee
and Long-eared Bats

On a fine day with the sun just bursting above the glossy, rustling leaves of the Pacific willow that sets its roots into the little seasonal stream skirting our property to the east, Susan is of the habit of taking her morning coffee on the deck that looks out over Satellite Channel toward Saltspring Island.

The coffee is Cuban, imported on the side by a tobacconist who specializes in fine cigars. Neither of us has ever smoked, certainly not twenty-dollar cigars, so precisely how she discovered her unusual source, I don't know and don't ask. But it's a superior coffee, this I do know.

She takes her book of the moment or the newspaper, which she seldom opens, preferring instead to savour the complex soundscapes created by the many songbirds that shelter in trees surrounding the house.

There are a stupendous broadleaf maple, a stand of old-growth Douglas fir, some massive Western red cedars that might be five hundred years old, and along the forest edge, all the deciduous opportunists: red alder, oceanspray, red currant, Indian plum, dangling vines of orange-flowered honeysuckle and dense thickets of thimbleberry and salal.

Some mornings the forest seems alive with bird calls. At times we hear the strange, musical sounds of our resident ravens. They resemble nothing so much as some avant garde duet. There can be the shrill *kleek-kik-ik-ik* of an eagle—a voice I've always thought a cruel joke on such a powerful bird of prey—and the peculiar clicking call of the pileated woodpecker, more often heard drumming on a tree trunk. Occasionally there is even the harsh prehistoric squawk of the great blue heron that visits to explore nesting possibilities in the treetops.

Red-shafted northern flickers swoop out of the forest, and on occasion one of the trees will fill with a cackling, cawing, scolding conclave of crows. It arrives for no reason that I can discern, stays for a round of muttering and grumbling and departs as suddenly.

But the real music comes from throaty whistles, liquid trills and quavering notes of the warblers and thrushes, finches and sparrows, wrens and chickadees, all punctuated by the occasional deep-toned thrum of an Anna's hummingbird zooming out of the woods.

The birds come down to the feeder suspended from a metal rod attached to the deck rail. The arm denies raids from squirrels or rats but swivels inboard for easy refilling. This ingenious contraption permits my wife to sit with her Cuban coffee and contemplate the politics of the bird world.

There is, for example, the bullying, squabbling gang of sparrows that scts up a din with its cheeping, twittering and jostling. A little pine siskin, drab and nondescript but for the flash of yellow along its wings, waits in a rose bush for a lull in the wrangling to dart in. A pair of American goldfinches comes and goes, unconcerned by the petty disputes around them. There's the house finch with its blush of red, the rufous-sided towhee with its chequered coat and distinctive red eye and the dark-eyed junco with its black executioner's hood.

Of particular interest lately has been a pair of red crossbills with the upper part of their beaks crossing over the lower, a marvellous bit of evolution that adapts them perfectly to levering seeds from the tight cones of evergreens.

The other morning I was just settling in to write when my wife, coffee abandoned, appeared in my doorway. There was, she said, an animal crisis. The sun was hot, so she'd been opening the umbrella on the deck. There was a furry critter in it.

I went up to look, teased open the folds and sure enough, there it was—a small, brown, trembling bat. We huddled for strategy. Ever try to get bat-handling advice on a Sunday morning?

Eventually, after a long string of referrals, she reached the SPCA's wild animal rescue centre. They were great: helpful, informative and really concerned for the safety of the little animal. Just open the umbrella and wait until it flies away. Why didn't I think of that?

The bat wasn't co-operative. As the umbrella opened, it crawled up and through the top vent to hang on the underside. Still, we got a great opportunity for close-up observation. It was, guessing from the extraordinary black hearing apparatus that projected well past its nose, an immature specimen of the nocturnal long-eared *Myotis*, a little insect-devouring bat that flits throughout the shadowy, mosquito-rich forest zones of the south coast.

Eventually our timid visitor took circling flight, making slow looping swoops in the unaccustomed sunlight, using its echolocation to deftly avoid windows, eaves, umbrellas and observers, before vanishing between the sheltering branches of the old maple.

The birds at the feeder were oblivious. I suddenly felt the same detachment from deadlines and a writer's other obligations, went back to my desk, hit the delete key and wrote instead this small morning dispatch from the real world of bats and songbirds and the simple, sustaining lives of trees.

The One that Got Away

Anyone who has spent time fussing over tackle boxes during winter downpours remembers the first fish.

If there are always bigger fish to be caught—or not caught—there's never one that will be more exciting. So a child's first fishing trip is always a momentous event.

My three-year-old asked if I'd take her fishing. I thought she meant the game we play sometimes. She dangles a string down from the loft and mum stands out of sight, attaches a trinket and tugs the line to squeals of delight from above.

No, she wanted to go fishing for a sea fish, in the sea. How could I not? The memory of my own first catch is as bright as the little nickel-plated spinners that were my treasure trove.

There wasn't a lot of money for frills in a household with four kids on a small-town sports reporter's wages.

My short steel rod resembled the poker beside our fireplace. The bait-casting reel had a star drag. It fouled line so effectively I developed a lifelong phobia. I haven't owned a star drag since. The monofilament line was a gift from my mother, squeezed out of the tight grocery budget. Lures I had to find for myself, retrieved from up and down the glimmering Nanaimo River.

I lived on—perhaps I should say in—that river for several sun-dappled years of my childhood.

My parents had just returned from a drizzly sojourn in England. After the dreary terraces and the terrors of a school founded on discipline, the pools and sandbars beckoned like the gates of Eden. From dawn to dusk, I spent my days there.

I came to know every riffle, hidden ledge, pool and sandy slough suitable for skinny-dipping.

Come fall, spawning salmon would seethe in the pool beneath our house, and then the big, seagoing trout would move in. After them came the serious fishermen. They had sheepskin wallets with flies in them instead of money, and real gear like split cane rods, wicker creels, vests with many mysterious pockets and single-action reels. They'd sharpen their hooks on a sandstone ledge. Some of them would watch the river for a while, then tie a fly right on the bank and start fishing.

One grim winter day, with the river in sullen spate and rain dimpling the surface, I encountered a tall man with waders, a tweed hat, a short tweed jacket and a long rod. He had a weathered, hatchet face with wrinkles around the eyes and a lick of longish white hair under the hat brim, and he spoke with the faint British accent of a man long in-country. He said he was fishing for sea trout.

I like to think it might have been Roderick Haig-Brown, but in truth it could have been any one of a generation of men who believed that a day stolen on the Cowichan, the Qualicum, the Tsable, the Puntledge or the Campbell would be a day of grace added to their lives.

He caught his sea trout, a silver torpedo with a yellowish belly, that made his line buzz and hum as it cut through the water. He held his rod high, the willowy tip even higher as the cane bent into arcs, bucking and thrumming as the fish ran and ran again. He was down to the backing when he beached it, then brought it up to the rain-slick ledge and asked if I'd like to learn how to clean a fish.

Oh, would I!

I got my first lesson in anatomy as he showed me its heart and gills and how to open the stomach to find out what a fish had been eating. He showed me a green woolly fly and how to tie a little spinner in front of it and suggested that might be a good way for a smart boy to catch a few fish. He squinted at me and asked if I swam in the river. I did. All winter long fishermen like him lost their lures on snags and log jams, he said with a twinkle in his narrow eye. A smart lad might set himself to retrieving a few for his own tackle box.

All winter I scouted the pools and log jams for the telltale glitter of lures lost the previous fall. Then, when summer eased the swollen current to a trickle, off I'd go to collect my tackle, splashing in like a puppy and diving for my prizes. Tee-spoons, weighted Mepps spinners, sometimes a small, silvery Deadly Dick: I found and admired them all.

After polishing, they went into the tackle box I pilfered from my school supplies. At Cedar Elementary, we kept our pencils stowed neatly in a wooden box. Mine had a sliding lid and a little brass catch. It was wasted on pencils.

I cadged a White Owl cigar box from the blacksmith at the top of our lane, made a quick switch one recess and put my precious spinners into loftier lodgings once occupied by HB, 2B and 4B pencils.

If Miss Soles noticed, she never let on. She loved her pupils and nurtured the small free spirits in her charge.

I may have graduated to a number 18 Adams dry fly and gone through the obligatory snobbishness regarding the lesser beings who use mechanical gear—it seems to afflict most fly fishermen—but I must also confess that it was one of those Grade 2 pencil-box spinners, trailing a caddis-fly larva picked from under a pebble, that caught my first trout.

It was an eight-inch rainbow that hurtled out of a chute of white water beside a tumble of logs. I fell in twice in my excitement, and when I brought my fingerling home in dripping triumph, my mother, a wise woman, set me a place at the head of the table where my father usually sat and fried it there and then. Some things cannot wait.

In the ever-changing life of a river, the place I caught my first fish is long vanished. The childhood tackle is lost once more except for one small spinner. My mother is dead. All are now washed away in some freshet of the relentless river of time. But a new generation has its own demands, so my daughter and I scouted our rods, selecting a powerful graphite that had been her grandfather's. We chose a heavy, red-sided lure that last fished the rips and currents of the Atnarko River at Bella Coola and we set out to catch our fish.

Heledd sat among a drift of little chocolate lilies and ate the picnic lunch—a big part of every fishing trip is the ritual—while dad cast the heavy lure into the powerful back eddy that curls behind a rocky point when the tide is on the flood or ebb through a narrow gut between islands. There was not much action.

I had half turned to explain that getting skunked is part of fishing when she dropped her cheese stick and pointed, mouth a perfect circle of astonishment.

Rising to the lure was the toothy grin of a mighty ling cod. It took the spoon with a great swirl and dived for the bottom, bending the rod double before breaking the line.

That was the last whiff of action. Yet if dad felt humbled by a lowly cod, little daughter was not. The thrill of her first fish still lay ahead. Meanwhile she savoured the other lasting gift that angling bestows. She scampered into the house:

"Mummy! Mum! Mum! You should have seen what got away!"

A Walk with the Rainy Sisters

The wind rose suddenly the other night, nudging me awake. It rustled through the forest canopy of maple and willow outside my window and snuffled around the eaves like some enormous, restless animal.

I slipped out of bed and into a pair of jeans, shrugged into my old Cowichan sweater with the snowflake pattern, stepped outside the world we parcel out in hours, minutes and seconds and went for a walk in the dishevelled vastness of time embedded in every starry night at the edge of the continent.

The wind had swept the sky clear. Stars glittered overhead in all their cold, indifferent splendour.

As I walked to the top of my drive, the wind sighed. Needles showered out of the trees, tickering against branches, a sound once used to describe flights of arrows in the *Iliad*. An owl hooted.

Not long ago I went up to retrieve the newspaper and discovered an owl perched on our mailbox. In the gloom I couldn't make out whether it was a common barred owl, a snowy owl or maybe even a rare spotted owl, although that's unlikely. Still, we considered each other gravely for several minutes, the bird's big yellow eyes never wavering. Then it ghosted away on pale wings.

This night there was not a glimpse of the shadowy hunter, just an otherworldly hooting off in the trees.

Above the road ran a river of stars, the Milky Way, the embracing arms of the galaxy, our home in the universe. I followed it westward, up to the hilltop where there's a small clearing with a picnic table.

The whole vista of the winter heavens spread around me. Way off to the west, in the glimmering distance above Cowichan Bay, Pegasus rode the horizon. To the southeast, above and between the habitation glows from Vancouver and Seattle, I saw the blue-white glitter of Sirius, the Dog Star.

Just above the southern skyline paced Orion the hunter and his two faithful hounds. Around me wheeled the double star Rasalmothallah, Cygnus the swan, Leo, Ursus Major and Ursus Minor, the navigator's star Polaris, Rigel, red-tinted Aldebaran and Betelgeus

It takes fourteen hundred years for light from Orion to reach us. I lay down on the picnic table and gazed into all that eternity. The light falling on me was shed in that far away constellation the same year that Pope Boniface IV consecrated as a Christian church the Pantheon, the temple built and rebuilt by successive emperors to honour the older gods of Rome, one more brief incarnation on its long journey into the increasingly secular present.

On the shoulder of Taurus stood the Rainy Sisters, sometimes called the Seven Sisters—Alcyone, Merope, Celaeno,

Taygeta, Sterope, Electra and Maia—the star cluster more properly known as the Pleiades, difficult to make out individually with my old eyes except on the clearest of nights, yet the same silent witnesses that shone their light on the great poet Sappho.

In the dark, I thought of her poem about the setting of the Pleiades, about longing and lost youth, a poem so sharp in its modernity that it still speaks to us across more than twenty-six hundred years. Her words have travelled even farther than the light from Orion, words that have moved a host of translators, perhaps the best of them Mary Barnard, born over a century ago in Vancouver, Washington.

Barnard was a lumberman's daughter from the wild, sodden forests of what Americans call the Pacific Northwest—though it is well south of our south coast—and as far from the tawny, sun-drenched Aegean Islands as one could be. But like Sappho, she fashioned the most luminous of poems. She wrote to Ezra Pound and to William Carlos Williams. They wrote back. She kept writing.

Her translation of Sappho has sold more than a hundred thousand copies. It has not been out of print in almost half a century.

Sappho remains a mystery. Maybe she was a wife and mother, maybe a courtesan, maybe a priestess. She's been claimed as an icon of gay and feminist literature, but the persona in her poems is ambiguous. She's been slandered by lesser talents and described by equals as matchless and unique. Her work inspired poets from Catullus to A.E. Houseman, from Ovid to Pound. It's said that in the library of Alexandria her work ran to nine volumes; today only fragments remain. Some were gleaned from quotations preserved by admirers or critics, others salvaged from the strips of papyrus torn from scrolls to provide inexpensive wrappings for the mummies of impecunious scholars in Egypt.

Poet and biographer Michael Schmidt wonders whether there might have been two Sapphos, the sacred and the profane, priestess and courtesan, perhaps conflated in the tides of memory. Perhaps she was both at the same time. "Lilac-haired, sacred, sweet-smiling Sappho," said her contemporary Alcaeus in a fragment quoted by Schmidt. "Her bones are dumb, her words outcry the tomb," said another.

What is certain is that she was a woman with a woman's sensibilities writing in a world of heroic cults infused with the warrior's ethos. If other women also wrote then, none of their work has survived. Hers did because her male contemporaries thought her poems incomparable and quoted them regardless of gender.

Mystery or no, Sappho looked at the Pleiades wheeling overhead one dark, starry night, as any of us may, and pondered, as do we all, the melancholy gyre of time in which we find ourselves spinning from youth toward eternity.

"Someone will remember us / I say / even in another time," says Fragment 147, translated by Ann Carson. And so we do remember her, by the light of the same stars. A chance to bathe in the same light as Sappho seems as good a reason as any to walk with the Rainy Sisters through a star-clad winter night on the West Coast.

The Power of the Tide

On the far horizon, trailing spume and vapours like some fiery chariot from a Greek myth, the blood-red sun plunged into the heaving darkness of the sea.

Everyone turned to stare astern.

The trimming of sails, the cleating and uncleating of sheets and halyards, the hoarse yelling of commands into a thirty-five-knot North Pacific gale, the ritualized choreography of making way in bad weather, all froze into a common stillness.

How many sailors since Odysseus have shared a similar moment?

Behind us, spindrift from its crest flying ahead to spatter against yellow Gore-Tex and taut white sails, another five-metre swell gathered, filled the view, seethed into the cockpit, then lifted the hull once again and hissed away beneath the rail. At that moment I sensed the organic muscularity of great mother ocean, how when you sail downwind, even a rough sea develops the slow swinging rhythm of the cradle.

And if the ocean is the cradle of life on this planet, its

simple rhythms permeate our lives, from the creatures that have evolved to survive in the sloshing and often hostile variables of a world between land and sea, to humans grown so distant from their biological origins that they sometimes forget them. Yet it might be argued that humans are inter-tidal creatures too. The regions governed by the tides are where we gather food, return to play and sometimes seek inspiration.

For all our urbanity, our high-tech jobs and our abstract educations, the ethernets and the stock exchange, the sea still shapes us in profound, perhaps unconscious ways. Our salty blood is an archetype from the primeval oceans that bore us. Beneath the gloss of commercialized sex and ro-manticized glamour, the ancient tides of human fertility wax and wane on a twenty-eight-day cycle that mimics the lunar pulsing of the sea. Sperm swim through a salty medium to their destination, and unborn babies float in a salty fluid. Even after eighteen years working away from my coast, I'd still wake to moonlight on the high plains, startled by the night wind trembling in the aspens, hearing in it the sound of distant surf.

Surfing cyberspace, playing at café society on Granville Island or choking in traffic during the rush-hour commute, we British Columbians remain a maritime people. All of us are governed by the pull of the tide in ways we seldom think about. Tides intrude into global commerce—governments worldwide devote extraordinary resources to monitoring and calculating the rise and fall of the oceans under the moon's pull as navigation aids—and they are part of our most intimate lives.

My own family still has furniture that rode the tides

around the infamous Cape Horn by sail. I once built a bookcase with bricks salvaged from a demolished house. Those bricks, I learned, had come from Liverpool as ballast, stabilizing a sailing ship through the boisterous South Atlantic, the Roaring Forties and the Furious Fifties—as sailors called those latitudes where the wind's unobstructed reach runs right around the world—then sold in a mining camp hungry for building supplies.

Homer's wine-dark sea is the same one that brings logs to Fraser Mills, takes pulp to Japan and wheat to China and brings back automobiles and mangoes and container loads of running shoes; that puts fish in the carriage trade restaurants and the latest laptop computers in the Future Shops. It's just as much the highway for Oona River and Ahousat—and scores of other small communities—as it is for oil tankers bound for Washington state's Cherry Point refinery complex or for Bremerton-based aircraft carriers and missile submarines capable of ending higher life on the planet.

For all our apparent estrangement, it seems we are not so far removed from those Sapperton dock boys who were prized as crew for the trans-Pacific windjammers when the fastest sailing ship ever built sailed from New Westminster. *Thermopylae*, home port Victoria, was bright green with teak decks. The polished-brass bulwark of her figurehead, sword pointing to the horizon, was Leonidas, king of the Spartans, who fell holding the pass against the Persians. Shining from her forward deckhouse was a gilded cockerel over the Latin motto that translates to "While I live, I crow."

As a clipper ship, she had much to crow about. *Thermopylae* was built to carry a thousand tonnes of high-value cargo at the greatest possible speed. Her canvas, all crowded aloft from mains to moonrakers, would cover an area the size of half a football field. Under full sail, *Thermopylae* heeled over until the deck rails were awash. Those sails generated power equal to that from a three-thousand-horsepower diesel engine today. Eight times, with a brisk wind on her quarter, the "bottle green clipper" covered distances in twenty-four hours that ranged from 480 to 531 kilometres. Once, near the end of her life, for three days while the wind held, she matched the CPR's express mail steamer, *Empress of China*, inbound from Yokohama at better than sixteen knots.

On her maiden voyage, the incomparable clipper made London to Melbourne in sixty days, Australia to Shanghai in twenty-eight days, Foochow to the Thames in ninety-one days. The London merchants fed her crew champagne for a week. These passages were never equalled under sail in maritime history. At the end of her life, the clipper served as a training vessel for the Portuguese navy but proved too much ship for the cadets to handle. On October 13, 1907, flying all her colours and with a military band playing in her honour, she was given a funeral befitting her namesake and sunk by a torpedo.

While registered in Victoria from 1890 to 1895, *Thermopylae* carried clear, close-grained timbers from New Westminster mills to Australia, Australian coal to China and rice from Rangoon to the BC mills that supplied Chinese miners and labour gangs building the railway. It's mostly forgotten now, but our first grain trade with Asia ran the other way, from there to here.

Too easily we fall into the Upper Canada myth

that the transcontinental railway is all that bound us to Confederation. Yet we know instinctively that it was not just steel rails, but men in wooden ships powered by the wind and hostage to the tides who first made possible that glimmering idea of a dominion that stretched from sea to shining sea.

A grizzled Greek mercenary was among the first. Apostolos Valerianos, called Juan de Fuca by his Spanish employers, was sent to find the fabled Northwest Passage reportedly sought by Sir Francis Drake in 1579 when he journeyed north after sacking Spanish ports in South America.

Marooned on the Venice docks twenty years after Drake's journey, the old Greek navigator is claimed to have spun yarns of a mysterious strait and a host of islands scattered across a spectacular inland sea. In 1596, despairing of ever returning, it was claimed he gave his map to Michael Lok.

The story's still disputed. Maritime historian Samuel Bawlf argues that Drake's real—and secret—mission was to find the Strait of Anian, or Northwest Passage, and that he sailed the BC coast but his explorations were suppressed for reasons of state security during England's conflict with Spain. It's known that Drake's brother was captured, tortured by the Spanish and imprisoned for many years in an attempt to obtain intelligence about Drake's journey.

According to the Greek pilot's account, he arrived on Mexico's west coast in 1587, the year before Drake would defeat the Spanish Armada on the other side of the world, and was assigned to pilot an expedition of three ships and 200 soldiers to find Drake's Strait of Anian and fortify it against the English. That expedition ended when the soldiers mutinied, he claimed. A second expedition in 1592 was successful, and he explored the strait and many islands before being driven off by warlike natives.

Was it dockside yarns and tall tales? Perhaps, except that the old pilot told Lok he'd know he'd found the strait by one striking landmark, a great spired pillar of rock standing in the sea around forty-eight degrees of latitude.

Captain John Walbran, skipper of the Canadian Coast Guard ship *Quadra*, commissioned in 1892, went looking for the fabled landmark at the turn of the century and, as far as he was concerned, found it. Captain Walbran, who later authored the definitive dictionary of coastal place names for BC, identified it as an unmistakable fifty-metre-high spire that juts from the sea near Tatoosh Island off Cape Flattery and that is now called Juan de Fuca's Rock.

Later, of course, came Cook and Hernandez, Quadra and Vancouver, Charles Barkley who named the strait for Juan de Fuca, the Boston men seeking sea otter pelts to trade in China, then the great burst of Asian trade that changed Victoria and Vancouver from fur-trade garrisons and mining camps to bulwarks of Victorian commerce.

Today British Columbians wax enthusiastic about the Pacific Rim and the vast market potentials of China, Japan, India and Southeast Asia. We ship grain and pulp and coal, import fabrics and exotic electronic goods.

In fact we only reinvent a mostly forgotten past.

The ghost of that dim memory of the first China trade lingers on the school grounds of Victoria, where one can still hear little girls on recess singing as they skip:

My ship came from China
with a cargo of tea,
all laden with gifts
for you and for me.

This skipping rhyme, which echoes the wonder of long-dead children who marvelled at oranges and lacquered combs, silk petticoats and fine porcelain, haunts the kindergartens of the West Coast.

Competition in the China trade was ferocious, sufficiently ruthless that today's business rhetoric about the exigencies of the New World Economic Order sounds like nothing so much as a description of the old economic order. Merchants would bid for the choicest "first chop" tea in Foochow market or top-grade wool from Melbourne. The first shipment to reach London commanded premium prices.

On May 30, 1866, *Ariel* and *Taeping* both slipped out of Pagoda Anchorage downriver from Foochow on a flood tide. After three months of continuous racing, they arrived off London only ten minutes apart. *Ariel* arrived first, but *Taeping*, with a shallower draft and a faster tug, docked twenty minutes earlier. Her captain and crew split their winnings with *Ariel*, which vanished at sea with all hands in 1872.

Captain M. J. Wright, retired from the China trade after a decade commanding the tea clipper *Leander*, wrote a nostalgic letter to the *Daily British Colonist* in 1892. He recalled the intensity of races twenty years earlier between the graceful sailing ships that had been consigned to the prosaic trans Pacific wool and lumber trade after the Suez Canal provided cheaper bulk transport by coal-fired steamship.

The tea market at Foochow had opened in the first week of June that season, he wrote. The first ship away was *Ariel*, followed the next day by *Lahloo* and his own ship *Leander*. *Spindrift* left a day later. Last away, four days behind the leader, was *Thermopylae*.

After eighteen days of beating down the South China Sea, *Leander* had caught *Ariel* and *Lahloo* and was first through the Sunda Strait that links the Java Sea and the Indian Ocean. Spirits rose. His crew was sure of being first to London, Wright remembered. But several days later, the steamship *Achilles* signalled that *Thermopylae* was gaining.

Leander's lookout spotted a sail on the distant horizon. By noon the next day, *Thermopylae* was alongside, and her crew mustered on deck to give three cheers as she swept by.

"How we looked to her, I do not know but she was the most magnificent picture of a ship under sail that I have ever seen," said Wright. "She truly walked the water like a thing of life.

"The next day at noon we could only just see her ahead. Later, I commanded the *Leander*, but in the 10 years I was in her she was never passed at sea, except by the *Thermopylae*, which, I believe is still the fastest sailing ship afloat."

The descendants of these tea races endure in the offshore yacht competitions like Victoria's renowned Swiftsure—the oldest continuously held race on the northwest coast—which pits high-tech vessels against the elements and each other.

Today's hulls are spun glass and laminated specialty woods, the rigging is stainless steel and space-age synthetics, and computers plot courses by satellite, calculating wind speed and the direction and intensity of currents.

But these are details. Boats are still sailed by men and women who can read a current from the wheel's kick and smell a change of weather on the wind; through these skills they remain on intimate terms with that past in which our common origins are framed.

It was to find a sense of that past, to get the faintest glimmer of what Captain Wright remembered, that I joined the crew of *Rage*, a famous twenty-one-metre offshore racer from Portland, Oregon. I found that some things do not change, no matter what the technology. Even the best sailors get seasick. Real sailing still means cramped and Spartan quarters, wet clothes and moments of fright punctuated by instants of unparalleled beauty.

From his place at the tiller, his short salt-and-pepper beard framing a face cured by wind and salt, skipper Steve Rander and I stared after that vanished sun, transfixed by the sudden radiance long after his crew had returned to its urgent duties.

I considered, then, how this small moment pointed to something bigger, to the romantic's heart that beat behind the tough, unyielding command presence so necessary to inspire a crew in the gruelling, fiercely competitive world of ocean yacht racing.

Steve Rander is a hard-headed Yankee boat-builder. Listening to him barking orders, I instinctively knew why he held the record passage from San Francisco to Hawaii in the Pacific Cup. He exuded competence. And mettle.

He explained how the perils of the sea consume the timid first, how the instinctive response in dirty weather is to reduce sail and slow down. "Better to crack on a bit more sail and drive through. The boat will handle better, and you'll feel more in control. Most people get into trouble when they underestimate their boats—they are built to take a hell of a lot more than we are."

A bit later the wind blew all the clouds away and then abruptly subsided. The moon was near-full. Black, foam-streaked swells sighed in the starlight. Above us the sails shimmered like apparitions.

I knew at that moment exactly what Victoria historian Ursula Jupp meant when she recalled the magic of the night of June 24, 1891, when the city of Victoria turned out at two o'clock in the morning to see *Thermopylae* scud home with a full moon silvering her sails.

"Perhaps it was also a harmony between the spirit of her first captain, renowned for his daring, and the beautiful lines of the ship that launched *Thermopylae* on the course that makes her still a legend among those who love to sail."

And, of course, a song on the lips of little girls who have never heard of the great ship, little girls who will grow up and teach the words to their own children, one more invisible strand that binds us to our seafaring past.

A Small Death at Whiffin Spit

The long bar of gravel named Whiffin Spit curves its white mile into Sooke Narrows, a maritime engineer's dream of the perfect natural breakwater. To windward, combers sweep in from Juan de Fuca Strait and spend themselves in creamy patterns on the shingle. In its protected lee, the glass-smooth channel forms a sharp gooseneck turn and spills into the broad basin of the finest natural harbour on Canada's West Coast.

Walk Whiffin Spit to its distant end, and you are really on a journey through time. The ghosts of history and prehistory hang as heavy here as the lowering sky over Possession Point. Just thirty minutes west of Victoria, with its manicured English gardens and double-decker tour buses, this stretch of coast bristles with Spanish names: Sombrio, Magdalena, San Simon, San Juan.

Except for the parking lot carved out to landward and the track where somebody once walked a D9 Cat a few hundred paces along the spit, the place has changed little since Lt. Manuel Quimper anchored his sloop *Princesa Real* here in 1790, rowed ashore and claimed the country for King Carlos IV.

The description in Quimper's log might have been made yesterday instead of two hundred years ago, although the massive pine beside which he buried the claim of the globe-straddling Empire of Spain appears to be gone—probably logged in the 1850s to feed the Muir brothers' sawmill.

"At the back of this pine the bottle with the document of possession was buried in the presence of all, the clerk whom I had named for this purpose certifying to it.

"I gave it the name of Revilla de Gigedo, had three salutes of musketry fired on shore, and one on the sloop of 21 shots. After having refreshed the men with very fine salmon berries and the kind of grape whose fruit is abundant, I went on board."

The historical evidence here runs deeper than the peremptory vanities of European kings, or even the three dead warriors of the T'Sou-ke nation that Quimper found, laid out with their wealth and regalia in three war canoes.

Strike out down the beach, and you cut through nature's record as well as man's.

A beachcomber's mossy salvage booms bob in the sheltered waters behind the spit. Higher up the beach, half hidden by waving seagrass and low scrub, lie immense hulks of timber we'll never see again, the silvery stumps of drift logs two arms' breadths across. Buried in the fine gravel that ridges the spit are twisted shapes of drift logs that came here on storms long before loggers made felled trees into neat cylinders with their double-bitted axes and long-toothed whipsaws. A more ancient ritual traces the high-water mark. Glaucous-winged gulls set up their raucous squabble for possession of the hook-nosed carcasses of beached salmon that have flushed out of the Sooke River. Loons and grebes cruise the back eddies waiting for schools of needlefish.

When I reached the end of the spit, where the outgoing tide roars, ripples and boils like a mountain river, I jammed my hands into windbreaker pockets and tried to contemplate the casual, mindless ruination of a place so beautiful.

The oil started coming in last week: heavy, gooey bunker-type crude, probably pumped out of some passing freighter's bilge. By the time I arrived at Whiffin Spit, the environmental authorities were calling it clean and had moved their major efforts farther west.

Clean is a relative term.

Six days later the oiled seabirds were still coming in— those that hadn't already sunk to the bottom as balls of tar. And people were still out there, taking time off work to walk the beaches without pay, trying to save little animals— which expresses something noble about the character of ordinary folk.

Ron Zakreski crashed out of the underbrush, arms full of oily merganser, and recruited the stranger to carry the bird while he drove hell-bent for the SPCA and a washing station thirty kilometres away in Victoria.

"We might save this one," he told me. "This one's got a chance. That's what we're here for, to give her a chance."

I looked down into that bird's bright, unblinking golden eye, the only part not matted with tar. It stared back in confusion and fear and failure to comprehend.

Oil oozed from the feathers, soaked into my jacket and dripped onto the car seat as we drove for Victoria and the rescue station. The bird gasped and fluttered, too weak to do anything but wait, powerless to avoid what might happen next. I looked into that frightened eye and forgot about Whiffin Spit and its wonderful past. All I could see was the future.

The next day, when I came back to check on the patient, I found that future in a small cream-coloured house on Napier Street just off Burnside Road in Victoria, the provincial capital. Up behind it, the clatter of mechanics at one of the city's biggest body shops continued uninterrupted, and traffic streamed steadily toward the nearby shopping malls, backing up at the lights, turning the air acrid with the scent of exhaust from idling engines.

Down in the crowded front room of the little house, where the oil spill death watch was underway, Robin Campbell waited for his patients to die. One by one, they meekly accommodated.

Campbell is a big, raw-boned specimen whose bulk hides the gentle manner of a man with the size to grow up fearless. He works with disabled people for a living and runs a volunteer organization called the North Island Wildlife Recovery Association.

The moment he heard an oil slick was washing up on the beaches west of Victoria, he took leave from work and drove the 150 kilometres south to help the SPCA set up the emergency cleaning station he knew would be necessary. He does the work without pay.

Oil afflicts sea birds in a number of ways. It fouls their feathers and reduces their buoyancy so that they must expend much greater energy to stay afloat. It destroys the natural insulating qualities of their down and exposes them to the strength-sapping cold of the North Pacific.

As they try to clean themselves by preening, they ingest oil, and it slowly destroys their vital organs. Some birds sink and drown. Others die of the cold, starve to death, get battered to pieces on the rocks or get picked up by beach watchers like me and come into the custody of the SPCA. There they wait to become statistics for Environment Canada and the BC government.

When I entered the Victoria cleaning station, Campbell was standing with his hands on his hips and staring into one of four makeshift pens. Warmed by heat lamps and covered by old blankets, the pens were jury-rigged from wooden frames and netting.

One pen was filled with terrified horned grebes. Other pens held loons, guillemots, murres, mergansers and some birds I couldn't identify.

The horned grebes huddled in a corner, the small miracles of their perfectly evolved feet scrambling for purchase on the unnatural footing, their crimson eyes darting and flashing.

But Campbell wasn't seeing them. His gaze said his mind was somewhere else, somewhere far away from this little doorway into a modern version of hell. I cleared my throat to announce my presence, and he started.

"They want 30 percent," he said to nobody in particular. "They want to save 30 percent." He reached into the pen and picked up a limp grebe, its brilliant eyes just beginning to glaze.

"I expect 15 percent."

He turned, held the grebe out to me. "That's the true picture of an oil spill. We just fed that guy. The energy it took for him to eat is probably what killed him. They're good and then they die. There's kidney and liver damage you can't see. In some cases the blood vessels explode. It's a horrible, horrible death."

The log book listed fatalities so far: 123 birds taken in, sixty deaths and another forty-five expected to die. It's an 85 percent mortality rate.

He led me to the back garden where a child's blue plastic swimming tank thrashed with murres, the diving birds that look like miniature penguins; their wings are adapted in a way that enables them to "fly" through water.

Those that can stay afloat for at least four hours stand a chance of being released. Those that can't will be put down, given the mercy of a fast death instead of a slow one on some beach.

Campbell netted a failing murre. "That bird's life is as important to it as your life is important to you. That bird knows it's dying. It feels pain and terror just like you. I wish everybody could come here and experience this. If there's one message we have to get across it's that life is not a bottomless pit. We just can't keep on doing this."

Somewhere beyond the horizon, the unknown ship that caused this obscene event motors toward the next port and its next "operational pump-out" of the bilges, heedless of what lies behind.

More than 70 percent of the oil slicks that foul beaches and slaughter wildlife are not spills but deliberate acts by ships' masters. And the problem grows relative to the marine traffic. Nobody knows how many seabirds are killed by exposure to oil each year, but the International Bird Rescue Center in California estimates at least half a million. But that seems conservative considering a 2002 study by Francis Wiese of Memorial University in Newfoundland.

Wiese found that more than 60 percent of dead seabirds recovered from Newfoundland beaches between 1984 and 1999 had oil in their feathers and calculated that at least three hundred thousand birds are killed by exposure to oil each year in Canada's Atlantic waters alone. Operational oil discharges continue to put millions of seabirds at risk, the researcher concluded. That's in Canadian waters, and on one coast, alone.

On the Pacific coast, there's not much research beyond the mortality estimates associated with the more dramatic spills that attract media attention—thirty thousand oiled murres and Cassin's auklets washed ashore in southwestern BC and Washington state after the widely reported spilling of eight hundred tonnes of Bunker C from the *Nestucca* barge in 1988.

But growing global demand for secure oil supplies inflates proposals for pipelines from the sedimentary basins of Northern BC, Alberta and the northern territories to a tanker terminal at Prince Rupert. The lobby for offshore oil drilling in Pacific waters intensifies. Cruise ships ply the Inside Passage, and container traffic from Asian markets floods into the ports of Vancouver and Seattle. So it seems likely that we'll see more small tragedies like the one at Whiffin Spit rather than fewer. It's estimated that more than thirty million litres of oil, gasoline and other petroleum products enter the oceans each year, more than half of it from land-based sources including storm drain runoff and improperly disposed-of motor oil. Of that total 20 percent is attributed to operational discharges associated with the routine maintenance of ships.

At least sixteen species of seabirds have nesting colonies

at five hundred locations on Canada's Pacific coast. The nutrient-rich waters support a population of 5.5 million including a stunning diversity of shearwaters, gulls, kitti-wakes, murres, auklets, murrelets, puffins, albatross and cormorants. Oil industry enthusiasts and those who beat the drum for development downplay the risk to wildlife. Yet the questions remain, unavoidable as an oiled bird flop-ping on the beach: how many seabirds face the grisly fate of those that came ashore on Whiffin Spit, and what's an acceptable mortality rate?

I asked about the oil-soaked merganser I'd carried in the day before, the one we thought might have a chance. Campbell looked up the bird's chart, riffling through the pages with his huge, blunt hands. He shrugged and spread them in a gesture of helplessness. One more small death to add to the tally from Whiffin Spit.

He fixed me with a wintry stare and paused for a long moment.

"Now it's the birds. Next it's you and me and my three kids. When are people going to figure that out?"

The Lighthouse Keeper's Daughter

Almost half a century ago, in a place far from this isolated, rain-soaked outcrop on San Rafael Island, itself a speck of rock off the remote west coast of Vancouver Island, there was once a lighthouse keeper's beautiful daughter.

She yearned only for the city she could see gleaming across the tide-torn channel.

Patricia Whalen was sixteen. As most teenagers might, she wanted only to escape the suffocating confines of parents and the sharply circumscribed world of the Entrance Island Lighthouse near Nanaimo.

"I couldn't wait to get off," she said.

Pat had moved to the little island, leaving behind her pals at the Chemainus school, when her dad sold the family's motel at Saltaire and took a government post as lighthouse keeper.

If Nanaimo wasn't quite the cosmopolitan Vancouver she'd come to love on visits to her grandfather, a retired Canadian Pacific Railway telegrapher who took her on walks through the exciting but slightly menacing urban landscape, she thought the Harbour City would suffice.

So when the sun made a burnished silhouette of Mount Arrowsmith in the west and night came spilling in over the Coast Range, when that velvet darkness brought to life the pulsing beacon that kept her father duty-bound, Pat would step outside and watch for her own telltale signal.

It was from Ed Kidder. The young fellow from Cedar had caught her fancy, but his long hair, slicked-back into the ducktail hairstyle favoured by bad boys—this was the 1950s—had failed to convince her parents that he was a suitable prospect for their lovely young daughter.

"His friends started to call him Jesus Christ," she told me, "because that's all my dad ever said when Ed used to come calling on me."

But Ed was determined. He would drive his old car down to the docks at Departure Bay and at the promised time he'd flash his headlights at the girl yearning across the water, a reminder that he was still there, waiting.

The moment that she was old enough, Pat shook off parental supervision, left her father's lighthouse and found a job with a freight company in Nanaimo. Not once did she dream that her Prince Charming, the young man who had been sweet on her since they were both fourteen, would abandon his beloved chariot, marry her and carry her off— to a lighthouse even more remote than the one she already thought of as a jail.

Pat told me their story as we sat at her kitchen table. Sheba the seven-toed seal-point Siamese was purring on the yellow tablecloth with the floral design, and the two family dogs were mumbling and grumbling underfoot while light from the million-dollar view poured in through the windows.

The young couple's first posting was to Gallows Point in Nanaimo Harbour, a cheery place that took its name from an execution there in 1853. But in 1961, not long after the birth of her first baby, they moved to Kains Island, just off the foreboding entrance to Quatsino Sound, a strange, eerie place that Pat still maintains is haunted.

Certainly Kains Island had the credentials for a neo-Gothic horror story, with a history of wives going mad from the isolation, lightkeepers drowning while children watched helplessly from the rocks and whole families almost starving to death when the supply ship failed to come.

"That's one of the things about lighthouses," said Ed, "the first person you meet is yourself, and you'd better like the company."

Pat remembered how her heart sank as the Coast Guard tender *Sir James Douglas* moved along the coast toward their new home. The dank, moss-covered rain forest crowded the high-tide mark, the heavy overcast pressed down, the days were closing in and everything seemed gloomier and gloomier.

"I thought I was going to the end of the world with a brand new baby," she said. "Now that place was isolated. It was the days before choppers. We only saw the Coast Guard every six weeks. We had a grave right outside our window. It was really spooky.

"We were so young. We were nineteen. Ed went up and introduced himself to the lighthouse keeper, Bob Collins, who looked at him and asked, 'Where's your dad?'"

But the principal keeper at Kains Island had a strategy for dealing with the loneliness.

"He had a movie projector and he brought in films from UBC," Pat said. "So we had our own film society. It was always a very formal evening. We all got dressed up and I put on high heels."

As was the custom for the junior man, Ed took the overnight watch—every overnight watch.

"We got fed up with the steady night shift," she said. "So I invited Bob down for tea to try to get him to agree to alternate. I thought I might as well be direct, so I said, 'Look, I'm a young woman and I'd really like to sleep with my husband occasionally.'"

The principal lightkeeper got red in the face and spluttered and blustered a bit, she said, but then thought it over and agreed to make the night watches a month on, month off proposition. Even with that concession, it did not seem like the optimum start to a marriage for the girl who longed for the bright city lights.

But life is full of strange twists and turns. She had Ed, and he had her, and that made up for just about anything that circumstance might throw their way.

"Yes," she said, turning to her husband during our chat, "we've been friends a long time, you and I. I must have had somebody looking after me, because I picked really well—although my folks had their doubts."

Looking back, she said she was grateful for the way it all turned out. Later she and Ed moved to Scarlett Point in the entrance to Queen Charlotte Strait and then to Carmanah Point, long before the now-famous West Coast Trail was resurrected from the old, once-abandoned Life Saving Trail built so shipwrecked sailors could walk to the outside.

They call it the Storm Coast. The Hurricane Coast. The

Graveyard of the Pacific. If Vancouver Island's rugged, fog-draped and rain-lashed western shoreline is the shield behind which the great population centres of the Lower Mainland and the Georgia Basin find protection from the raging weather of the North Pacific, it's also where the bones of more than two hundred shipwrecks lie strewn among the reefs, shoals and rocky headlands.

It's to protect mariners along this dangerous and inaccessible lee shore—twenty-seven thousand kilometres of ragged coastline stretching from Puget Sound to the Alaska Panhandle—that the Canadian government maintains one of the world's most extensive networks of lighthouses, lighted beacons, buoys that monitor weather conditions and wave action, and other aids to navigation.

Tough, resilient, resourceful, inured to isolation and privation, frequently the first responders in marine rescues, the lighthouse keepers like Ed and Pat might also be said to represent British Columbia's vanishing coast, the last of the tiny outports where lives are connected to the outside only by sea, air and the radio.

They put up with storms and weird sea conditions and their own mistakes—getting caught short of rations when the tender is late, for example.

"Once we were down to a case of Prem and a case of canned peas, some rice, some soda crackers and some mustard," Pat said. "That was all we had left to eat. We never went short again though. I stock my pantry now. I've had my own 7-Eleven store in the pantry ever since."

In 1968 Ed decided to move his family closer to town and took a position as the second principal keeper at the Sand Heads in the mouth of the Fraser. But they found something had changed. Pat no longer pined for the bright lights she could now visit whenever she desired. And Ed didn't like the station much either.

"There used to be a lightship at the Sand Heads," Ed said. "They replaced it with this box on pilings off the end of the Steveston jetty. I was going to quit the lights then. I went down to the office to resign and they said, 'We have this guy at Nootka with health problems.' He wanted to be closer to a doctor. So we just did a straight switch."

Which is how, in 1970, the Kidders found themselves returning to the island's isolated outer coast with their son, Dean, eight, and daughter, Nicalena, five.

"They loved it here," Pat said. "They were really glad to get out of town. This is a pretty sacred place. Before we moved here, I had gypsy feet and I always wanted to move on. But I hit this place and I just wanted to stay. I feel blessed that I've been able to live my life on my own terms."

Her "blessed place" is a small house below a red and white concrete pillar that is buttressed by a steel frame. It's strong enough to withstand the hurricane-force winter storms that sweep over this craggy islet with its dense salmonberry thickets and shore pines sculpted like bonsai by the ceaseless wind.

Behind it the beach, carved by tide and weather into a perfect crescent moon, is the safe anchorage to which Mowachaht mariners directed Captain James Cook in 1778 with the cry "*Nutka-sitl! Nutka-sitl!*"—"Go around! Go around!"—which the explorer mistook for the name of the place.

Its real name is Yuquot, a term derived from *yuk-witte*, place of wind, and *aht*, the people. So this is the ancestral home of The People of the Wind. That wind and the surf it piles up into towering swells are constants here at what Spanish and British explorers named Friendly Cove.

To get here, you can drive west through the mountains from Campbell River to Gold River, then catch the coastal freighter *Uchuck III* down Muchalaht Inlet on one of its re-supply trips to the West Coast outports and work camps. Or you drive from Nanaimo through the mountains to Tofino and charter a float plane to carry you on the seven-hundred-dollar flight northwest along a coastline of seething reefs, deep sea caves hollowed into the cliffs by booming swells and blinding white beaches of crushed shell and sand.

The sea under sunshine is a stunning palette of blues, greens and aquamarine, although it can quickly change to the colour of polished pewter or a sullen grey, all squall lines and fog sliding away to silver-flecked cobalt and ultramarine over the deeps.

If you're lucky, you'll see the spout of a sounding whale, a raft of sea lions or a huge black bear foraging on one of the tiny creek estuaries.

To come here is to travel into a past that still intrudes into the present. History permeates this place. In the little cove outside the Kidders' kitchen window, Captain John Meares built the first ship on this coast, the schooner *North West America*.

The vessel's capture by the Spanish, who built a fort with gun platforms on San Miguel Island right outside the Kidders' back door, triggered the Nootka Incident that brought the empires of Spain and Britain to the brink of a global war and shaped the northwest coast into what's now British Columbia.

And on a grassy isthmus now occupied by the last Mowachaht family to live here—the rest moved to Gold River when a now-defunct pulp mill offered jobs there in the mid-1960s—once stood the longhouse where Chief Maquinna entertained Captain George Vancouver and Captain Juan Francisco de la Bodega y Quadra at a dinner that helped defuse the growing tension.

But the past that really intrudes is even more ancient. It's a solitude governed by the great cycles of the seasons and the weather. The sea and the storms that contort its face are still the gods that rule here.

Pat and Ed did not imagine, when they arrived back on the wild edge of the continent—where even with satellite dishes and helicopter pads, the rhythms of life are closer to the eighteenth century than they are to the twenty-first—that their sojourn would last so long.

But they spent almost thirty-five years at the Nootka station—a time so long that Pat would become a fixture to mariners and a legend in her own right as the throaty, reassuring radio voice that crackled out of the spume and spindrift late at night to lend comfort to the lost or nervous or to lonely sailors keeping the middle watch.

"Pat Kidder," they tell you, "the Lady of the Lights."

And neither guessed that Ed's exploits saving mariners in distress—more souls saved in his career than in that of any other keeper on BC's Pacific shore—would make him an icon for crusaders on the West Coast who insist that the bean counters, bureaucrats and brass hats in Ottawa who argue that lighthouses could be run more efficiently by robots and remote control are dead wrong.

Between 1996 and 1998, arguing that modern maritime

navigation equipment permits the automation of lighthouses, Ottawa renewed a program of destaffing. Eight lights were destaffed and automated.

The program was shelved when a storm of angry protest erupted down the whole coast. This place, protesters pointed out, is more than container ships and blue-water tanker traffic. There's a whole inshore small-boat culture that knits together coastal communities and their economies.

"We've been to the ropes with this bunch three times now in the past sixteen years," Ed said. "They say major shipping no longer needs manual lights. But in our time on the Nootka light, the interaction and communication between the keepers and the public has increased about a thousand percent.

"On this station particularly there's been a tremendous number of search and rescue incidents, and there have been hundreds, literally hundreds, of preventative incidents that never get reported. It's a matter of being available."

Search and rescue teams in the Pacific Region respond to hundreds and often thousands of calls involving land, sea and aviation incidents each year, and lighthouse keepers are often the first to respond.

One of her proudest moments, Pat said, was listening to fishboat deckhands, tugboat skippers, crabbers, boom tenders and the others who wrest their dangerous living from the sea. They had come in from twenty-seven coastal communities to tell representatives from "The Outfit," as Ottawa's Coast Guard brass is known out here, that it was crazy to take human beings like Ed and Pat off the light stations.

"They said [of Ed], 'I wouldn't be alive if it weren't for that man standing over there.'"

Those are telling compliments here on the Graveyard Coast, where you can't look at a chart without finding the symbol for a shipwreck. George Nicholson, a maritime historian who sailed the west coast of Vancouver Island for the first half of the last century, records 241 known wrecks and seven mysterious hulks of unknown origin.

The victims range from warships like HMCS *Galiano*, lost with all hands off Triangle Island in November 1918, to the New York sailing packet *William Tell*, which foundered near Carmanah Point two days before Christmas in 1865.

Around Nootka Sound, not counting the sacking and burning of the American trading vessel *Boston* by Mowachaht warriors in 1803, among the early recorded wrecks are the sailing ships *Lord Western* in 1853 and the *Iwanowa* in 1864.

And then there are those that will never be identified— a sailing vessel burned to the waterline that First Nations people say came ashore near Estevan Point some time before 1870, for example. Or the iron gunboat from an unidentified navy that rusted away for a century near Tsusiat Falls. Or the origins of the hulk buried in the sand at Long Beach and thought to have been there for at least 150 years before Nicholson mentioned it half a century ago.

The wreck of the *Valencia* was one of the most horrific maritime disasters in Canadian history and the first grim consequence of Ottawa's policy even then of shortchanging the West Coast of lifesaving facilities, writes maritime historian Donald Graham in his book *Keepers of the Light*.

When the *Valencia* struck a reef off Carmanah Point in the bitter January of 1906, horrified observers ashore watched helplessly as she broke up in the surf just thirty metres away while 123 of her 154 passengers and crew—many of them Americans who had desperately clambered into the rigging—were finally swept away to be drowned or pounded to death on the rocks.

When an enraged US government demanded answers, Ottawa struck a commission, and its recommendations led to the building of the isolated lighthouses strung down the whole outer coast of the island. One of them was the Nootka station, built five years later in 1911.

"The country has three oceans, but in Ottawa they seem to think it's the Great Lakes and the Rideau Canal," Pat said. "We're really fed up with bathtub admirals coming out of Ottawa and telling us there's no further need for lighthouse keepers."

More recent marine incidents may not have the headline value of the wreck of the *Valencia*, she said, but they are no less urgent for the people involved.

There was the garbled, difficult to understand call from a crab boat. Ed guessed the boat was off Descubierta Point and went out with his son, Dean, in the station's inflatable. In the middle of the night, with the sea and sky merging into each other and everything as black as India ink, they found a Vietnamese family's crab boat.

In the boat's cabin they discovered a surreal scene. Six members of the family lay comatose in the late stages of carbon monoxide poisoning. They got them out into fresh air and called in a helicopter. One elderly woman died during the medical evacuation, but five were saved.

There was the local priest, Father Frank Salmon, whose pastoral duties take him from Ahousat to Kyuquot, undoubtedly one of the wildest parishes on the planet. "He called and said he was sinking." Ed went out to the rescue.

There was the *Doughboy* coming out from Gold River when it struck a deadhead and capsized near Escalante Rocks. At the Nootka lighthouse, the radio suddenly erupted.

"You sit there and listen to the panic and the fear in the voices," Pat said. "This is the sort of thing I wish these dumb-asses in Ottawa would figure out, but they don't seem to have the imagination to even go there."

It was three o'clock in the morning, raining and so dark that in lowering the station boat from its davits, Pat couldn't see the water and left Ed dangling a metre above the surface while she wondered why he kept yelling against the wind and wouldn't start the motor. Ed said he reached the area three hours later, knowing that in the cold water conditions, his biggest enemy was time.

"I knew that if those guys were in the water, they weren't going to last very long. I thought we were going to be looking for dead bodies." But then his light flashed on something in the darkness, Ed said. "Thank God for those cruiser suits with a reflective strip on the shoulder."

"There were four guys, and they were one life jacket short," said Pat. "One guy said he'd go without. 'I'm young,' he told them. 'I don't have a family, and you all have kids.' There he was, a young guy, ready to die so his crewmates' kids would grow up with daddies—that's the kind of people we're talking about."

Ed found two men on the upturned hull and another on a floating fish box. He pulled the fourth man from the water thanks to that reflecting shoulder strip.

It's for selfless acts of bravery like this that BC's indefatigable Senator Pat Carney flew west to present the Kidders with the Queen's Golden Jubilee Medal in a ceremony at the Coast Guard's Pacific headquarters in Victoria.

"I think I've learned more about life here than any place I've ever lived," the woman who once longed for life in the city told me. "I've had some real mind-blowing experiences up that beach. The wind, the sea and the sun, the eagles, the whales and the ravens"—she paused to point—"the other day, right out there over the cove, ravens were doing this dance.

"And over there"—she pointed again—"a wolf pack came out. We watched them playing in the tall grass, just playing, their rumps in the air, for about twenty minutes until they vanished back into the forest. When the herring spawned, we had eight whales, sea lions, every tree had an eagle in it, every tree a raven. It's like the whole world comes back to life in herring season. It's been my university."

As we talked, around us lay all the litter and tumult of a household in transit. For after thirty-four years on the Nootka light, after forty-two years of keeping mariners safe, the longest service of any lighthouse keepers on the West Coast, the Kidders are finally moving Pat to town.

Sometime later in the day, they'd be closing the door to the trim red and white house next to the light tower for the last time. They'd bid farewell to assistant keeper Jack Douglas and his wife Glenda and the fragrant beds of tulips and daffodils, bluebells and morning glory—even a splendid rhododendron—that Pat lovingly terraced into the lee of the storm-buffeted house.

The goodbyes to her neighbours—Ray and Terry

Williams, the last Mowachaht family living at Yuquot across the cove, Janet Etzkorn way down the coast down at Carmanah Light, the folks at Estevan Point, the only place in Canada shelled by the Japanese in World War II—those goodbyes had all been said.

And I had no doubt they'd be holding hands as they made their way down the long gangplank that Jack's been sprucing up while they prepared to embark upon a new life in the domesticated tranquility of Qualicum, a growing retirement village just north of Nanaimo on the mild and sunny east coast of the island.

I can predict the hand-holding with certainty. Spend a day with the Kidders and one can't help but notice how often their hands touch in that intimate, unconscious expression of affection that comes only to old, old lovers.

"I've got a dishwasher in this house I'm moving to," Pat deadpanned. "I don't know how to use one. I only got an automatic washer after the kids had left. I've never used an ATM machine and I'm afraid of them—they can eat your card, can't they?"

"But I really want to learn to drive a car. I'm really good in a boat. I just don't know how to drive a car. I'm confident enough in a boat because then it's only me and the sea. In a car, I'd be worried about all the other drivers."

She tells how she was once down in Victoria with her friend Janet. They were walking back to the hotel from a drugstore at midnight when she was transfixed by the peeping and warbling of a flock of birds she'd never heard before. Janet laughed.

"She said, 'They're not birds, Pat, that's what they put on the crosswalks for blind people.'"

Pat was pulling my leg a bit here. One thing that wise folk learn·to appreciate in the long, dark months of a winter on the lights is the value of a good sense of humour. But there's a more sober side to this too, even a touch of apprehension.

"We started as kids and now we're old crocks. All the principal keepers I ever worked for are dead," Ed mused.

Pat nodded. "The world that we left is long gone. I worry about how we'll deal with the new one. What if I get over there and find everything is just so predictable and quiet? I never wanted to leave here. Everybody in the Coast Guard thought I'd die here. But I said to Ed, we'll know when it's time to go. Everything will fall into place. And now it's here. The ravens danced. It's time to go."

A Brief Visit to the Other World

I am sitting on an upturned bucket on the splintering, bleached-out government dock at the mouth of the Kingcome River.

The icy torrent's colour, a silty sheen disturbingly reminiscent of the milky hue of an old blue eye gone cloudy with cataracts, signals its source in the immense ice fields of Silverthrone Glacier. But I'm contemplating instead the innumerable shades of grey that texture a West Coast fog bank when it rolls in beneath a winter overcast that seems as heavy as a sodden wool sweater.

I've had plenty of time to do this. Before I noticed, my cell phone had discharged its battery by searching for service that's not there. Even my watch begins to feel like a useless artifact left by a time traveller from some unknowable future.

Mist rises above the estuary. It mingles with the drifting tendrils of fog. Somewhere I can hear the muffled *kiik-kik-kik* of an eagle, but the tree where the regal bird roosts is just a vague shape.

Behind me open aluminum runabouts bang and clatter against boom logs. Gumbooted young men clamber in and out of these tinnies, the only means of transportation to the small village hidden beyond an upstream bend. The small aluminum boats raced down the fast-moving river, dancing around the snags and gravel bars, skittering sideways over the boils and whirlpools of the current, then shooting a narrow gap into the slick water behind boom logs anchored to keep the dock clear of flotsam.

Kingcome, our name for the village where Margaret Craven set her great novel of death, discovery and deliverance, *I Heard the Owl Call My Name*, is so ancient that Kwakwaka'wakw creation stories say it was founded right after the great flood that anthropologists believe marked the end of the last ice age. That would be about fourteen thousand years ago. To the Tsawataineuk people, whose ancestors were here millennia before Abraham made his name as a Biblical patriarch, their ancestral village is named Gwayee.

Ancient pedigree and famous literary reputation or no, like many of the other little outports scattered among the labyrinth of islands and fjords that notch British Columbia's central coast, the village is connected to the outside world only by sea lane and float plane—and that final, treacherous bit of river.

Getting to the outside and back is nothing romantic for those who have lost family members to the fourteen-kilometre round trip on the river. Or who have had someone bleed to death because the river was frozen and impassable, as it was for Dennis Willie's grandmother Emily. She died giving birth to his mother two days after Christmas. That happened many years ago, but the pain endures.

Since 1965, I'm told, thirty people from Kingcome lost their lives because there was no road. Some families lost successive generations. Emily Willie's own sons, Frank and Ernie, later drowned in the icy river. Imagine thirty people lost from a village of two hundred—that's 15 percent of the population.

I've that in mind as I watch the fog through the dissipating clouds of my breath and consider the contrast between this place and the temperate bubble of altered reality that sprawls from Vancouver to Seattle. It lies maybe three hundred kilometres south, as the crow flies, but a lot farther than that as a journey through perceptions of time and cultural sensibility.

Bustling through the manufactured environment in their steel and plastic commuter pods, the urban folk listen to blustering talk-show personalities on the radio or to Avril Lavigne on the iPod or get texted last-minute instructions on their BlackBerrys about picking the kids up after school as they head to and from the climate-controlled office towers from which they may nip out for a double espresso whenever they like. So easily do they forget that there's another entirely different world out there beyond the city limits.

Vancouver wallows in a narcissistic infatuation with being a world-class city. Victoria preens in the imagined gentility of a romanticized Victorian past. Yet British Columbia is also a province of remote outports, isolated places like Kingcome in which two planes at the dock are a traffic jam and the elements are not an inconvenience reported on the Weather Channel—they rule your life.

In this other-worldly BC, people are forced to pay attention to the great cycles of sky and sea, tide and tempest, the subtle semaphore of fog banks and the messages that clouds write on the horizon. Nature alone determines when you come and go, not the bus schedule or the boss's decision that everybody has to be at a workstation by nine o'clock in the morning.

Just up the float, bush pilot Wayne Podlasly is chatting with the locals about the prospect of something happening with this weather. He wants just one decent hole in the cloud through which his battered old Beaver might ascend in one of those tight spirals that coast pilots must master if they want to fly in a world of towering mountains, narrow valleys, clag and spindrift and spume.

Wayne tells me he has been a pilot for thirteen years, the last seven on floats. He's been a roofer, had a snowmobile business, even run his own flight school at one point. He prefers the challenge of flying the inlets and the scattered outports that depend on his bush plane the way city folk depend on the taxi. Medical emergencies, family visits, flats of preserves from distant grannies, logging crews, visiting dentists and the odd jar of treasured eulachon grease all are part of the coastal pilot's normal payload.

"What I like most about this is that you get to be part of the community," he tells me, handing out string-wrapped parcels and swapping salty gossip with the young guys loading the village freight into their tinnies.

I'm philosophical about delays, myself. I'd begun to prepare myself for a long one the day before when I looked out the kitchen window where I was staying and saw the fog slowly rolling and boiling down the channel toward Echo Bay in the Broughton Archipelago between Vancouver Island and the continent.

By evening we were socked in tight. Yet the next morning I got surprise notice from Mark Alexander, an old friend who sold his house in Surrey, dumped his desk job and went back to his roots as a North Island bush pilot.

Pacific Eagle Aviation, the outfit Mark now serves as dispatcher, had a Beaver in the area and would be happy to pick me up and drop me back at Port McNeill—if I didn't mind tagging along with the freight on the rest of the mid-coast freight run.

There's a saying that guests, like fish, start to stink after three days, weather or no weather. This was Day Three at Echo Bay, time to move on. So I gratefully hitched a ride.

"There's going to be a lot of up and down because of the fog," Wayne warned over his shoulder as I attempted to jam myself into a back seat already overwhelmed by the essentials of the outports—mailbags, a new computer for some kids at Wakeman Sound, somebody's new outboard motor, a whole entertainment centre, a new chainsaw, crates of chainsaw oil, the electric piano that had to be delivered in time for a Kingcome Inlet birthday party.

Wayne seemed oblivious to my increasingly frantic hunt for the seat belt buckle beneath sacks of Her Majesty's Mail, still rattling on about the dirty flying conditions ahead of us.

"Nothing to worry about, though, as long as I've got turn radius, and I've always got my back door open," he said. "This is just life for a pilot on the coast, I guess." By back door he meant the clearing weather behind us—I hoped.

He pointed at the headphones hanging beside me. As he brought the throttle back and the cockpit drowned in the engine's throaty roar, I quickly put them on. Blessed silence. Sort of. Now I was listening to the laconic, often cryptic chatter between the pilot and his dispatcher.

We took off, sort of, skimming along between fog and sea. First stop, Wakeman, where the radio informed him there was a hole in the clouds so that, after his drop, he could get up over the fog bank. Unfortunately, by the time we'd unloaded, the hole had moved and was blocked by a large mountain. Now there was sunshine on the water over Belle Isle, so we scooted over there—but the hole was too small. Wayne shook his head in disgust. The ceiling was getting lower.

"I'm just going to follow the coastline. It will take me right to the government dock," he said.

We took off again, floats not far off the water, ready to set down again in an instant, everybody keeping eyes peeled for deadheads and floating debris.

Massive cliff faces loomed from the mist just off the wing tips. Then, just as abruptly as it had seemed to lift, the fog settled again, flat on the glassy water. The radio announced there was bright sunshine over Kingcome Inlet.

So Wayne taxied—the rest of the way up the fjord.

"Can't do this with a plane on wheels," he grinned. Right. And what, I asked, if we meet a big seiner while we're taxiing through this soup?

"Nah, they've got radar. They'll move. When you get up on the step and you're really moving, that's when you might have to worry," he said.

And so we arrived at Kingcome, having taxied the whole way. The sunshine had fled. Nobody was moving except the young guys gunning their boats for a river mouth that

I couldn't see. They could probably find their way home blind at midnight.

Suddenly Wayne is scrambling to get us back into the Beaver. There's a nice hole opening right above the dock. In minutes we're spiralling up through layers of murk. Seen from above, the inlet looks strange, magical: a ghost river of fog sliding between the mountains. Mist boils up into rounded, puffy tops of the kind that Victorian artists imagined for angels, illuminated by shafts of golden sunlight that tint them with mother-of-pearl.

Unfortunately there's now heavy fog over Port McNeill. Maybe we can get home by flying underneath it. Over Wakeman Sound, he banks steeply and slips through a hole. There's good visibility, but not out in Queen Charlotte Strait. As we fly west, the ceiling gets lower and lower, and Wayne decides to turn back. The hole over Wakeman behind us has just closed.

"Mark is just run ragged in this weather, eh," the pilot chortles. "Everything is backing up now."

But there's a more pressing problem. The Beaver's fuel is down to eighteen gallons, not enough of a margin to chance going home and having to divert. Now we're on a gas hunt.

Coming off Wells Passage, we set down in the fog. As the ceiling rises, we get off the water; when it suddenly lowers again, we touch down again and taxi. Up, down, up, down, just like a roller coaster. But the fog clears at Sullivan Bay, a float camp where, serendipitously, we have a bag of mail to drop, and they have a pump and aviation gas.

Wayne fills the tank and we're off again, hurrying now as the winter dusk closes in.

"It's pretty bad, man. I'm going to try to blast off and go through that hole at Wakeman," he tells the distant base. "Or shall I go the long way round and try to find a hole on Johnstone Strait?"

With perhaps twenty minutes of daylight left the radio crackles. It's the dispatcher.

"I can see Sointula," Mark says. "There's cloud on top of Malcolm Island. Looks like fog behind on your side. Real clear over here."

Just then a hole pops open over Sullivan Bay and we're up, through the grey and just as abruptly bound for the glittering lights of Port McNeill, only fifteen minutes away when you're up here, a whole century away when you're down there in the fog—and from the Big Smoke, as Vancouver is known in these parts, an entire world away.

Glass Sponges
and Jurassic Reefs

Eyes straining to see down a fan of light that frayed away in the all-encompassing primeval darkness, Kim Conway stared as a ragged white line began to emerge like distant ghosts from the eternal night.

Above him a column of water the height of a fifty-storey skyscraper crushed down on the little two-man Delta submersible he shared with his pilot. Beneath its keel, the muddy plain of the ocean floor still showed the marks scoured by glaciers more than twelve thousand years ago.

Yet for the moment, the Geological Survey of Canada scientist—whose mundane office at the Institute of Ocean Sciences on Vancouver Island's Saanich Peninsula overlooks a drab parking lot—was less interested in the physics of the ocean bottom that the awesome sight he was witnessing.

As the miniature submarine drew closer, the fringe of white became a fantastic, subtly coloured landscape that was knobby with fronds and fingers, cones and boot shapes, fragile tubes and delicate fluted structures that still evoke a sense of the magical, even from the still photos that popped up to greet my visit as JPG and GIF files on Conway's of-fice-bound computer screen.

These were sponges, part of a huge series of reef struc-tures that cover more than seven hundred square kilo-metres of sea floor between the Queen Charlotte Islands and the mainland and in Queen Charlotte Sound off the north end of Vancouver Island. Several similar colonies of the fragile creatures have since been found off the east coast of Vancouver Island, the Gulf Islands, West Vancouver and the Sunshine Coast, but the unparalleled immensity of the formation on the undersea Fraser Ridge off the mouth of the Fraser River is of particular interest to scientists.

All are extremely vulnerable to damage by fishing, re-source exploration and the laying of power or communica-tions cables. Yet living structures like this were once be-lieved to have been extinct since the end of the Jurassic, the age of the eighty-tonne brachiosaur and toothy allosaur, the fearsome meat-eating prototype for *Tyrannosaurus rex* that even then was tall enough to look over a suburban house.

In an age of giants, the reef sponges once formed the largest biotic structure the planet has known, a single com-plex that was seven thousand kilometres long—more than three times the length of Australia's Great Barrier Reef—and spanned the ocean shallows between what's now North American and Europe.

Land masses then looked nothing like the familiar continents of today. Warm, shallow seas were home to ichthyosaurs and long-necked plesiosaurs. In one of these seas, named Tethys by paleontologists and geologists, glass sponges like those found off the BC coast massed so thickly that they left deposits ranging from 120 to 400 metres thick;

the most prominent are along the northern rim of the Alps. But fossil outcrops from this reef have since been found in the Caucasus, the Black Sea, Romania, Poland, Germany, Switzerland, France, Spain and Portugal, off Newfoundland and in Oklahoma.

For some reason, although the individual species continued to exist, the gigantic sponge reefs vanished from the oceans after their maximum about 145 million years ago. And for some equally mysterious reason, they re-established themselves in BC waters at the end of the last ice age.

"It was like finding a living dinosaur," Conway told me when I dropped by a Patricia Bay office cluttered with computers, deep-sea specimens and a midden of papers, loose-leaf binders and books. "It was like looking through a window into the past. We've talked to hundreds of geologists worldwide, and nobody has seen these kinds of reefs elsewhere."

For Conway, the research dive in the summer of 1999—a joint venture with scientists from the Institute for Geology and Palaeontology at the University of Stuttgart in Germany—was really the culmination of a quest that began a decade earlier with some squiggly lines on a graph.

In the mid-eighties, he said, a survey that mapped hazards on the sea floor turned up a weird anomaly. Where the seabed should have been flat, sound waves bouncing off the bottom showed peculiar bumps rising nineteen metres, the height of a six-storey apartment block.

Researchers later confirmed that the mounds were not a geological structure but were actually composed of living organisms. They were hexactinellids or glass sponges, so named for their skeletal structure. Glass sponges extract silicon dioxide dissolved in water and from it create for themselves skeletons fused from a delicate lattice of glass strands. Specimens of individual sponges can be up to four metres across but are brittle and will shatter, well, like glass, when struck by trawl gear, sports anglers' heavy downriggers or prawn and crab traps. Nobody knows what impact seismic testing for undersea oil and gas might have on them.

The reefs off British Columbia's north coast are thought by scientists to extract from the sea water an amount of silica equivalent to fifty-seven thousand railway cars just to accommodate overall growth for a single year. On an otherwise featureless ocean bottom, the complicated shapes of the glass sponge reefs play another important ecological role: they create habitat that's widely used by many other deep-sea creatures.

What Conway had been looking at through the submarine window was the thin mantle of life formed by the newest generation of sponges, each layer built upon the skeletons of its predecessors in a sequence that reached back unbroken for at least nine thousand years.

In 1991 the young scientist and three of his compatriots—Vaughn Barrie, John Luternauer and Bill Austin—published a paper about the discovery. However, other projects demanded time and resources, and the research went into hibernation.

Then, in the mid-nineties, one of the world's leading paleontologists read their paper about the north coast find. Manfred Krautter, a scientist at the Institute for Geology at the Leibniz University of Hanover, had been studying the ancient fossil reefs in Europe. "This is the only place we can see living examples of these fossil reefs," Krautter told me enthusiastically when I tracked him down years later at a 2008 scientific symposium. "It takes nine thousand years to grow them and ninety minutes to wipe them out." With his interest and scholarly authority, the international Sponge Reef Project was born and led to the submarine dives in 1999.

Their discoveries included the fact that these reefs provide a nursery for baby rockfish that take refuge in the crevices between sponges. Given the pressure on rockfish populations, that's particularly significant. But in truth, little is known about the ecological role the reefs play.

The federal government moved to close areas immediately surrounding four significant reefs in Hecate Strait, but by then much of the damage, some of it likely irreparable, had already been done.

"Large areas are abraded, fragmented and ploughed as trawling doors and weighted nets impact the sea floor," the researchers wrote in a paper published in 2001. "The brittle sponges cannot withstand this mechanical stress and break and crumble. This ultimately leads to the death of sponge individuals and to the reduced opportunity for recolonization of the affected area."

In fairness, bottom trawlers voluntarily tried to avoid the reefs after 1999, and shrimp trawlers voluntarily stopped fishing there in 2000. Inadvertent damage continued, however, and there was finally a regulatory gear closure for bottom trawlers over the reefs in July 2002. It was tragically late.

"Maybe only 30 to 40 percent of the reefs are still in a pristine state," Conway told me ruefully. "The trawl impacts will take, we think, perhaps fifty years to recover." Krautter was more pessimistic when I talked to him. He thought half the reefs in our marine Jurassic Park, some fluted, some whorled, others ornate and calyx-shaped—this astonishing wonderland of creatures once thought extinct—might have already been inadvertently destroyed through ignorance, carelessness and bureaucratic lethargy.

A New Spit at Oyster Bay

A sullen Strait of Georgia chop hissed over the beach pebbles and slopped along the drift logs lining Oyster Bay as I huddled against the sleet in my squall jacket, dry but bitterly cold.

Still I was thankful for the chance to stretch my legs while I waited for Gordon McLaughlin to make his way from Willow Point near Campbell River.

This little bay was once a booming ground for timber coming out of the Iron River watershed. The loggers are mostly gone, but the black stubs of old pilings still scar the mudflat.

Not long ago the shallows were smothered by rotting bark chips. Now there's a rich carpet of seaweed. As I watched, a bald eagle settled on something, to the raucous dismay of seagulls and crows.

McLaughlin, who's lived near here for more than half a century, is one of those guys who pays attention to what's happening around him.

He showed me a series of small but troubling changes

he's been cataloguing, wondering whether they might be harbingers of global warming and its unanticipated effects.

McLaughlin led me on a brisk walk down the beach, first past a jumble of rain-slicked logs, then through slippery clumps of seagrass and finally out past rubble that was once part of a low breakwater shielding log booms from storms.

I stopped briefly to turn over a piece of rusty steel, a fragment of HMCS *Matane*, which was scuttled here to extend the breakwater. It was an ignominious fate for the frigate to which Hitler's entire Baltic fleet surrendered.

But it wasn't the work of man that McLaughlin wanted to show me. It was the work of nature: a new spit curling out from the point, sandy beach filling in behind and pebbles, unyielding as road pavement, packing in on the outer side.

"Six years ago, the spit wasn't there," he said. "Now it's huge. It's twice as wide this winter as it was last winter. It's tripled in size in a few years."

Then he took me to the far side of the bay. Half of an old service road next to the beach had washed out, and the main road wasn't much more than a car length beyond.

He cited other weird little signals that something is happening.

"Kelp beds—they are disappearing. The kelp bed between Hernando and Savary Island has disappeared," he said. "On the other hand, something has kicked the local prawn production sky high. People are limiting out on one pot where they were once finding it difficult with several."

What's causing these changes? He doesn't know.

Maybe logging on the upper Oyster River a few kilometres south has overcharged the watershed with silts and gravels, changing the flow and consequently redirecting the current once it reaches tidewater.

Maybe it's a result of the small rise in sea level—between one and two millimetres a year—already attributed to global warming. Increases of that magnitude are imperceptible to most of us, but McLaughlin wonders whether, coupled with high tides and winter storm surges, they might be enough to affect low-lying foreshores.

"We've been watching for signs of ocean rise," he said. "We've noticed some surprising changes—subtle, but definitely there. The first signal was the sudden creation of the spit at Oyster Bay. The second was erosion on Tyee Spit [in Campbell River]. Third, we've noticed that drift is thrown much farther [up the beach] during storms."

Then he pointed across the strait.

"There's one hanging glacier over there on the Coast Range that's kind of our marker. It's showing black rock in the centre for the first time."

Maybe it's incremental. Maybe it's all these things combined with tiny changes in wave patterns as a consequence of changes in wind direction and tidal configurations. During storms, McLaughlin said, there appears to have been a ten-degree shift in the prevailing wind direction in front of the house he's lived in for thirty-four years. Would that alter wave patterns?

Whatever it is, perhaps, like him, we should all pay closer attention to the natural world around us, looking for the little signs that nobody seems to notice but that may yet accumulate into the big effects that nobody can ignore.

Tsunami

The next time you are visiting downtown Vancouver or Seattle, look up at the tallest building you can find on the skyline. Now imagine a black wall of water about twice that height rushing toward you at initial speeds of 160 kilometres per hour.

That's what three salmon troller crews faced on the night of July 10, 1958. They had anchored for the night in Lituya Bay, Alaska, when an earthquake and landslip generated a wave 531 metres high.

Technically it wasn't a tsunami but a swash, the violent sloshing of displaced water in a confined space. Whatever one wants to call it, geophysicists know how high the wave was because it scoured the mountainsides, leaving only naked rock.

Howard Ulrich knew only that it was higher than any wave he'd ever seen as it roared down on his 11.5-metre boat *Edrie*. With him was Sonny, his seven-year-old boy. Anchored a little farther out were Bill and Vivian Swanson aboard *Badger*. Orville and Mickey Wagner crewed *Sunmore*.

In an interview forty-two years later, Ulrich told the BBC that it was like experiencing an atomic explosion. "Like the end of the world," says a laconic Coast Guard rescue unit transcript.

Miraculously Ulrich's boat remained afloat. The other two craft were hurled treetop-high over a spit and into the open ocean where *Badger* foundered. Somehow the Swansons survived. The Wagners and their boat *Sunmore* simply vanished.

I was thinking about that wall of water and what it signified for our assumptions of permanence while looking across the white-flecked seascape into Cowichan Bay from my vantage point on Lands End at the northwestern tip of the Saanich Peninsula.

On a crisp, clear, cold afternoon, with pale sunlight silhouetting the snow-clad mountains of Vancouver Island behind, the blue January shadows stole out to cover the broad flood plain of the Cowichan and Koksilah rivers as quickly as they must have done 305 years ago.

That was long before Captain James Cook sailed up the outer coast and almost a century before captains Quadra or Vancouver arrived in the wrangle between Spanish and British empires over who had the best claim to the northwest coast.

In that time before our written history on this coast began, powerful Cowichan chiefs from the six villages of the valley would have been enjoying the full seasonal swing of ceremonies that still take place during Siset, the long winter moon, the coldest time of the year. Spirit dances would mean visits between villages, feasting, dancing and singing that went on late into the winter night

On one of those nights, something happened that would imprint itself upon the oral histories that are indigenous peoples' collective memory. We know because an eccentric British professor—to the amusement of many contemporaries and the present contempt of those whose cultural enlightenment enjoys the benefits of a century of hindsight—began collecting stories from the Cowichans around 1902.

Charles Hill-Tout's work was edited by Ralph Maud and republished by Talon Books in 1978. After sunset, his informant told him, the ground began to shake. The shaking lasted twenty hours.

"It was so severe that it made all the people sick, threw down their houses and brought great masses of rock down from the mountains. One village was completely buried beneath a landslide. It was a very terrible experience; the people could neither stand nor sit for the extreme motion of the earth," Hill-Tout's informant says, the source as evocative today as it was then.

Documents from Japan recording the date of a tsunami, analysis of trees that died suddenly between August 1699 and May 1700, physical evidence of foreshore disturbances and mathematical models calculating in reverse from the tsunami's point of impact in the western Pacific all leave scientists confident that an immense earthquake off Vancouver Island rocked this region at about nine o'clock in the evening on Tuesday, January 26, 1700.

How powerful? Powerful enough that it entered the oral histories of people up and down the coast. Sometimes the stories are almost reportorial. Sometimes they are rendered in mythological terms—whale and thunderbird fighting, or sisiutls, supernatural two-headed sea serpents associated with temblors and floods—in the same way ancient Greeks associated Poseidon, both sea god and earth-shaker, with earthquakes and tsunamis.

Ruth Ludwin, a research scientist with the Pacific Northwest Seismic Network and the University of Washington's Department of Earth and Space Sciences, has researched these fascinating accounts. She's assembled numerous references that describe the kind of event remembered so vividly by the Cowichans.

Ludwin discovered that from the Yurok, who live on the Oregon-California border, to the Tlingit of the Alaska Panhandle, the stories all mention inundations, loud noises and shaking.

The Klallam of Washington state tell of river valleys flooding at a time of year when it was so cold that survivors froze. The Huu-ay-aht of Bamfield on Vancouver Island's west coast tell of longhouses being swept off the beach. The Nuxalk of Bella Coola tell of people fleeing to the mountains when the sea rose to drown entire villages. There's a Tlingit story of a supernatural being that lives beneath the sea, and when disturbed, sends giant waves. The Makah tell of the sea withdrawing and then rising so high that some who escaped in canoes drifted ashore north of Nootka, far to the northwest on the outer coast of Vancouver Island, where their descendants still live.

One Cowichan story collected by Hill-Tout recalls "a noise like the report of a great cannon" after which the river rose rapidly although there was no rain. It rose so high that drift logs were cast on mountains. When it subsided, "all the animals had been drowned and . . . the fish had died;

there was nothing for the people to eat but the bodies of the drowned animals or the floating fish."

This sounds like what tsunami survivors in Southeast Asia might have faced if the Indian Ocean great tsunami of 2004 had occurred before satellite communications could flash images around the world and before jet aircraft could move disaster response teams to the stricken area in days.

One Nuxalk story, collected by anthropologist T.F. McIlwraith more than seventy years ago, includes an intriguing mention of a "white man's anchor" found high above the treeline on Mount Kwatna, about sixty-five kilometres west of the present townsite of Bella Coola on British Columbia's mid-coast.

If this sounds far-fetched, there is evidence of seismic shocks generating tsunamis of mind-boggling size. Some have been civilization-shattering events that dwarfed in impact even the disaster that unfolded in Thailand after the 2004 event.

A recent book, *Tsunamis in the Mediterranean Sea: 2000 BC–2000 AD*, by a team of Russian scientists from the P.P. Shirshov Institute of Oceanology and the Institute of Marine Geology and Geophysics, sifted evidence for hundreds of marine seismic events.

Among them was the fate of the Minoans. Almost thirty-four hundred years ago, the seagoing empire from Crete was the United States of its day, an unchallenged mercantile superpower. Almost overnight it vanished. We know this from the bewildered records of its chief trading partner, the Egyptian empire, which indicate that, from one week to the next, Minoan ships simply stopped arriving.

As early as the mid-1920s, a French seismologist wondered if it had fallen victim to a huge tsunami. Now geophysicists, archeologists and scholars of classical literature piece together a jigsaw puzzle that strongly suggests he was right.

About 1380 BC, geophysicists confirm, a volcano at Santorini in the Aegean Sea blew up. The explosion was four times bigger than the eruption of Krakatoa. Excavations on Crete show damage to buildings that seems consistent with the powerful suction of withdrawing water. All around the Mediterranean rim there's further evidence of flood damage that reached three hundred metres above sea level.

Meanwhile classical scholars cite a report by ancient historians that Troy was flooded around this time. And a papyrus surviving from Egypt's Eighteenth Dynasty reports chaos, darkened skies, "an unceasing boom" and entire cities destroyed when "water came from the north, rose as a huge flow and flooded the whole country."

The Russian scientists speculate that Egyptian scribes were describing the shockwave from the Santorini blast, heavy falls of ash and the great tsunami that obliterated the Minoans and possibly many other city-states in Greece and Asia Minor.

Are our modern, high-tech civilizations still vulnerable to such events?

Well, one volcano in the Canary Islands is poised to shed half a trillion tonnes of rock into the Atlantic. That could send tsunamis higher than the tallest skyscrapers into the lowlands occupied by cities like New York, Boston, Washington and Miami. Here on the West Coast, Hawaiian volcanoes have a history of similar collapses. The last occurred 120,000 years ago. As recently as 1792 a smaller volcanic cone collapsed at Shimabara, Japan, where a wave like the one at Lituya Bay killed fifteen thousand people.

"Virtually all oceanic volcanoes grow, become too steep and slough off flank materials," wrote Steven Ward of the University of California's Institute of Geophysics and Planetary Physics in the February 2002 edition of *Nature*. He estimated that a collapse of the volcanic cone of Kilauea on Hawaii would release the equivalent of a 4,100-megaton blast and send twenty- to thirty-metre tsunamis—similar to those that devastated Asia—against North America's coast.

Vancouver Island shields the low-lying Fraser River delta from the kind of tsunami that swept away the Huu-ay-aht so long ago, but there's danger in the sheltered waters between the mainland and the island too.

A number of submarine landslides have occurred in the Strait of Georgia in historic times, say researchers from the Geological Survey of Canada. Other scientists have mathematically modelled the consequences of an underwater slump along the steep face where beds of Fraser Valley sediments drop off into deep water at Roberts Bank. They predict that, under the right circumstances, a tsunami more than twenty metres high could be discharged against the eastern sides of Mayne and Galiano islands.

Not a monster like the ones that devastated the ancient Mediterranean, destroyed Shimabara, thundered out of Lituya Bay and reshaped the oral histories of aboriginal peoples, perhaps. Still, it could be sufficient to give us pause for thought, considering our continued propensity for placing a real estate premium on walk-on beaches and concentrating dense urban populations in low-lying flood plains and in river estuaries.

The Last Donkey

If some Labour Day you should happen to hear the whistles of a steam donkey echoing off the hillsides just south of Campbell River, it won't be a ghost from the long-gone camps of Mac and Mac, the Elk River Company, Iron River Logging or Grassy Bay Timber.

It will be the genuine item, a ninety-year-old piece of equipment from the days of whistle punks and misery whips, lovingly restored as a working artifact for the district museum and proudly asserting this Vancouver Island town's claim to be the genuine heartland of coastal logging.

It's now more than fifty years since I made my initial journey to the town that still lives and breathes the burly, sweat-stained mystique of the logger, and I'm the first to acknowledge that bold declaration might be disputed by folks from the Alberni Valley or Port Alice.

But it remains the kind of place where you will stop for a beer at the Quinsam Hotel and encounter some geezer with stagged pants, carpal tunnel syndrome and more ruts than a rainy-season logging road who tells you gleefully that the Campbell River hospital is the best place in the world to get treatment for a bad chainsaw cut.

So it was no surprise that when the museum staff first got up a head of steam in the restored donkey for a test run, men from all over town made a beeline for the source of a sound that hadn't been heard for more than fifty years.

"When people heard that whistle blow, they just came running," museum director Lesia Davis told me with a laugh. "The mayor heard it from his office and he was here in a flash. You should have seen all the beaming faces around that steam engine. I realized—it's the ultimate boys' toy!"

The steam donkey is much more than that, of course. It also represents a period in history in which the face of BC was utterly transformed.

At the turn of the last century, logging was a brutal, back-breaking occupation in which men felled trees with axes and crosscut saws and used ox teams or massive draft horses to skid the logs to tidewater. Most operations were restricted to within a few kilometres of the shoreline.

A typical camp a century ago might stuff forty loggers into a bunkhouse three deep. Often the bunks were "muzzle-loaders," jammed so tight men had to crawl in from the end. And while bosses romanticized them as places where happy men played the fiddle and sang around a pot-bellied stove, the loggers complained of "dirty straw, vermin, wet clothes steaming and stinking around the central stove, little ventilation, no privacy or means of cleanliness."

Mind you, the loggers themselves were not exactly saints.

Consider the fall afternoon when Prohibition came

into force province-wide in early October 1917. When the shift whistles blew, three hundred loggers converged on the Willows Hotel to—in the understated words of the *Comox Argus*—"bid John Barleycorn a fond adieu."

Lillian Williams later described the soiree from the point of view of the wives, mothers, sisters and daughters who gathered on the hill out back to keep an apprehensive eye on their menfolk.

"The loggers smashed their glasses and bottles on the tiled floor as they emptied them until everyone was wading and sliding around in broken glass. This degenerated to throwing glasses and bottles at one another," she recalled. "In the short space of two hours that evening, the loggers broke up the tables and chairs, smashed the windows and tore the doors off their hinges. The bar was saved from total destruction when the crowd expanded to a free-for-all brawl which moved outside in the open."

By that time the steam engine was already changing logging and its culture forever. The first locomotive went into action on Valdez Island in 1901. By 1917 ninety-eight of them were at work on sixty-two different logging railways in BC.

The donkey engine replaced the ox teams that skidded logs out of the bush. Like many technologies, it at first mimicked what it replaced. A single cable could drag logs more quickly than animals, but horses would then drag the cable back into the bush for the next load.

The first donkey engine arrived at Duncan Bay in 1903. A logger named Wallace Baikie recalled years later how it arrived by raft with a full head of steam, ready to winch itself ashore. However, the crew that came to the beach didn't know how to set the new rigging and decided their familiar horses should pull it ashore.

When the pop valve blew, bleeding pressure from the boiler, men and horses alike bolted for the treeline and refused to come out, convinced it was about to blow up.

Soon a haulback system was devised for winching cables back to the logging show, and that was the end of the horses, which went the way of pit ponies at Cumberland, Nanaimo and Ladysmith coal mines. Next someone realized mounting the donkey on a flatcar would extend the reach of the loggers. Before long, railways were laid in the valley bottoms, and while thousands of steam donkeys puffed and squealed up and down the coast, steam locomotives hauled the massive old-growth timber to the booming grounds. The donkey engine and spar tree became symbols of logging.

The steam donkey at Campbell River was built by Empire Manufacturing in Vancouver in 1916 and worked on West Thurlow Island and Glendale Cove before finally being left to rust at the head of Knight Inlet. It was brought out by the local Rotary Club and a forest company, and the painful four-year work of restoration began.

"It was rough," Lesia said. "We would have to scrounge and make calls to old-timers. Sometimes a part would come from Port Hardy. Sometimes it might come from the bush. We might have to make it ourselves."

But if the steam donkey that now rests and occasionally rumbles outside Campbell River's museum represents a romantic past that recedes to the unravelling fringe of living memory, it also reminds us of the astonishing speed with which technology emerges, transforms our lives and then subsides into obsolescence.

In just forty years, trucks would replace locomotives, and the ubiquitous steam donkey, rusting away in the bush, would follow the horses and pit ponies into industrial oblivion. The forest industry had moved from muscle power and pork bitches—chunks of fat skewered on a stick and burned to provide light—to helicopter logging, grapple-yarders, feller-bunchers and computer-assisted sawmills in less than a century.

Summer of Fire

It's just after daybreak. Numinous rays of early sunlight slant through the canopy far overhead, plunging between the grey tree trunks to disappear into the glossy green salal and the whispering sword ferns.

Among the salmonberry thickets and thimbleberry canes crowding the fenceline of adjacent farm fields above the Oyster River estuary, about midway between Courtenay and Campbell River on the east coast of Vancouver Island, a choir of songbirds raises a boisterous hymn of praise for the morning.

The cathedral-like quality of this small corner of forest at the estuary of the river was doubtless what first attracted the tough World War I chaplain from Vancouver's East Side who sought solace and solitude here with his fly rod. The riverside Padre's Trail commemorates him.

Watching a big cutthroat trout as long as my forearm hang motionless in the swift, clear current, I'm reminded of that long-dead angler and his pastoral meditations. He must have been an optimist. He may have fished for souls on East Hastings, but for his own peace and salvation, he returned to this temple of nature so often that he finally became part of the geography.

If this seems an unusual place to begin a contemplation of the trial by fire through which British Columbia passed in the summer of 2003—which recurred in 2009 and will doubtless visit again—perhaps it's not.

For this rich oasis of tranquility, throbbing with life, is the future of all the devastation around Kelowna, Kamloops, Cranbrook and Lillooet that so shocked our urban officials and those television news directors who have an insatiable appetite for the dramatic but bring little historic memory to their coverage. Those ravaged landscapes might also serve as images from the past of this place of present abundance.

In 2003 Lieutenant Governor Iona Campagnolo described the summer's losses as "agony." Premier Gordon Campbell, after flying over the burns in the Southern Interior that are expected to cost the province $500 million in fire suppression, said the desolation seemed "endless."

Almost everyone who owned a television could not help but be mesmerized by the images of blazing forests. As flames menaced suburban neighbourhoods, the steady mantra from television sets declared British Columbia's worst summer of fire in fifty years. And who could not feel the deepest of pangs for the suddenly homeless?

However, like most things in life, it turns out to be a little more complicated than the television newsrooms claim.

Agony is a relative concept rooted in emotive human values. Considered on a different scale, what's indisputably painful to the people who lost their possessions to wildfire is simply part of the natural life cycle of a forest. And that forest exists oblivious to the humans who often share its landscape without fully understanding or respecting the natural forces that maintain it.

This assessment of our collective ignorance and lack of respect is not an arbitrary opinion. It's clearly expressed in a research paper published in the spring of 2003. The paper sought to assess the degree of risk to which we've subjected our urban fringe areas by meddling in natural processes. That risk is growing rapidly, the scientists concluded. Unless federal, provincial and municipal governments move swiftly to develop a comprehensive strategic plan, we're going to suffer more such tragedies. They may reach catastrophic proportions where what's now called the urban-rural interface expands along the fringes of growing population centres.

To acknowledge the remorseless nature of fire in the wild is not to diminish either the suffering of those who fall victim to its whims or to be parsimonious in our sympathy. It is to recognize that the world is complex and that events have different meanings in different contexts.

As the lovely forests around the Oyster River attest, the scorched earth that so shocked British Columbia's premier and television audiences is anything but endless. Indeed, the fecundity at which I'm looking beside the Oyster is what those wastelands of ash and cinders in the Interior will become.

For within living memory this too was once just such a wasteland. What's known as the Oyster Flats was once devoid of vegetation, burned to the bare ground, even the topsoil consumed in the inferno.

Today most of this is second-growth forest. It grew up

again after a pair of horrendous forest fires swept through the region in 1922 and 1938. As with the mesmerizing fires in the Interior, the flames swept away villages, homesteads and farms in the twinkling of an eye. And just as they did in the infamous summer of fire, politicians solemnly pronounced upon the gravity of the calamity.

Fire, it turns out from even a casual reading of history, is a fundamental part of life in this vast province where immense forests cover almost two-thirds of the landscape. It's not just part of the physical reality, it's part of the mythic structure of our identity, a psychological icon we hold in common with other Canadians.

Uncontrolled forest fire sweeping out of the wilderness to destroy our notions of civilization is a recurring event in Canadian history. Since detailed statistics began to be kept in 1908, there have been more than five hundred thousand fires in Canada big enough to be worthy of record.

Every year the mischievous genie escapes again from the bottle to defy our belief that we are in control of nature rather than the other way around.

Perhaps we secretly welcome the fury of the fire season. This helps explain why it has such enduring news value, even when a distant blaze threatens a scattering of log cabins in some place most Canadians have never heard of and will almost certainly never see.

For one thing, wildfire subverts the order of our planned and scheduled existence. It serves as a confirmation of true impermanence in a world attached to the illusion that everything deserves a guaranteed and desirable outcome— medical treatment, consumer purchases, employment, education, material possessions, life itself.

One might conclude that 2003 was indeed the worst fire season in half a century—if you happened to be one of the unfortunate people whose home was destroyed or if you measure in terms of area burned by individual fires. Turn to other scales of comparison, however, and the desperate summer actually fell well within a historic pattern.

The exhaustive tabulations of federal and provincial agencies that maintain databases on wildfires suggested that the much belaboured summer of fire was actually right on the annual average for BC.

For example, counting since 1970, the average number of fires expected in BC's forests each year is about twenty-five hundred. In 2003 the total number of forest fires recorded to early September was marginally less than the average at 2,468. In 2009 there were slightly more fires recorded by late August, but they had burned less than half the territory of the fires six years earlier. Yet in 1994 there were more than four thousand fires. In 1908 there were only 835 fires reported in all of Canada—but one of them was among the most destructive in BC's history.

The difference, some will argue, is that 2003 and 2009 were worse because so many fires occurred near human habitation, threatening even urban residential districts and creating thousands of fire refugees. That too is an assertion that's open to interpretation.

The fire season certainly looked worse, thanks to television and modern communications. Yet delve into the history, and even the two summers of fire look not so bad by comparison to catastrophic fires that have swept BC's forests in the past.

Forest fire has erased whole cities from the map, not just

outlying residential neighbourhoods. More than a thousand buildings were destroyed in the city of Fernie in 1908. Heat was so intense that the steel wheels of ore cars melted where they stood. Four years before that, the town of Hosmer had been destroyed by fire.

At least ten people perished in the Fernie fire. The toll would have been greater had not coal miners skilled in disaster response calmly helped hundreds of potential victims escape by train just before the worst of the conflagration. And while fires in 2003 and 2009 have tragically claimed the lives of a few firefighters, the victims of fires in the past have numbered in the scores and in some cases—like one dreadful 1894 fire in Minnesota—five hundred or more who were incinerated on their farms and homesteads.

Some fear this past is becoming our future. The interface is growing between forests and the residential fringe of towns and cities. Subdivisions that promise tranquil suburban security expand into the surrounding hinterland. Increasingly urban residents embrace the presence of trees and wooded areas as a value that enhances the aesthetic quality of city life.

The problem for our urban society is that fire is a natural, recurring and even essential part of forest ecology.

As a consequence, the costs of fire prevention and suppression will increase and not decline with growing population—a point that the research for the Canadian Forest Service emphasizes and to which BC's auditor-general has drawn urgent attention.

Ecologists have long understood that most tree species are evolved to take advantage of fire and that periodic wildfires actually contribute to forest health. Fire is a process that maintains biochemical equilibrium, releasing for other uses the chemicals and energy otherwise bound up in vegetation.

Diseased, dead and dying trees are cleansed from the forest; new browse and habitats are created for deer, moose, caribou and their predators; insect infestations are suppressed; the opening of the canopy permits light to reach the forest floor, and new plant species enter the cycle; the burning of clutter and debris on the forest floor ensures the next fire will not burn too vigorously; even the chemical residues of burning serve to fertilize and regenerate large parts of the ecosystem.

There has been a long-standing conflict between this holistic view of forest processes and a cultural view in technologically intensive western societies that fire is an enemy that competes with us for industrial feedstock and threatens our living space, and therefore must be fought and vanquished. The latter view may be understandable, springing as it does from a long history of tragic encounters with forest fire by largely helpless settler populations. Yet preventing fires which would otherwise reduce the long-term accumulation of fuel in forested lands is now seen as the source of many of our emerging risks. This is particularly true for the urban fringe where subdivisions bleed into wilderness areas. As the recent destruction in BC's interior demonstrated, there's good cause for concern, especially at the fringes of conurbations like Vancouver, Victoria and Seattle.

For much of the past century, governments fought fires with a fervour that approached a holy crusade, complete with propaganda campaigns led by Smokey the Bear. Foremost, of course, was the threat wildfires posed to human habitation—and few would argue with that necessity. But fire suppression has more often been pursued in the interests of a forest industry that didn't want merchantable timber damaged or because fire-scorched landscapes are unpalatable to an urban public increasingly removed from the natural world that equates the process of wildfire with destruction rather than renewal.

University of British Columbia forestry professor Michael Feller was warning the Greater Vancouver Regional District a decade ago that fire-prevention logging in watersheds like those on the North Shore could actually increase fire hazards.

Feller pointed out in 1992 that coastal old-growth forests are less of a fire hazard when left unlogged, while forest plantations can be a greater risk because their uniform growth height makes them susceptible to crowning, a phenomenon in which wildfire races across the treetops, igniting the canopy.

In their natural state, old-growth forests can sustain repeated burns of less intensity. The thick bark and great height of mature Douglas fir, for example, enable them to withstand fires that quickly consume debris and smaller trees; this process makes future fires less destructive by depriving them of accumulated fuel.

Two or three metres up the trunks of some of the surviving old-growth trees here along the Oyster River, the scorch marks of ancient fires are evident—including the Big Fire of 1938 that swept down Vancouver Island from Campbell River to Courtenay. It burned an area roughly fifty kilometres long and twelve kilometres wide. By way of comparison, that single fire burned an area twice as big as the total area burned by more than thirty-six hundred fires in 2007 and 2008 combined.

The Big Fire was just one of many blazes that have transformed the landscape. Researchers like Stephen Pyne, who studies the history and culture of wildfires, observe that we live on a "fire planet" in which almost everything is in some state of oxidization. Indeed, the process that yields fire is also the process that makes animal life possible. Fire predated human existence. Our entire time on the Earth has been one of both adapting to it and adapting it to our purposes, from learning to cook food in the Paleolithic to slash-and-burn agriculture in Australia and the Amazon and from prairie grass fires ignited by Plains tribes to the recent technological culture of fire suppression in the service of economic and aesthetic interests.

Scientists mapping the extent of prehistoric fires found that during the century between 1550 and 1650, for example, a chart of the burned area covered a significant portion of dry southeastern Vancouver Island. Yet when loggers felled much of the old-growth Douglas fir at the beginning of the last century, many of the trees had been standing for hundreds of years before those fires of the Elizabethan era.

Today scientists like Reese Halter—president of an Alberta-based international forest research institute and co-author with University of Victoria ethnobotanist Nancy Turner of the recent book *Native Trees of British Columbia*—increasingly argue for a fundamental change in our attitude toward forest fires and how we log.

Instead of fighting all fires with fanatical zeal simply because they threaten commercial values on public land or to assuage the public's sensibilities regarding the view in a park, we should be much more selective in identifying where to fight and where not to fight wildfires.

Obviously fires that threaten human life and habitation, as did those in the Okanagan and the Kootenays this summer, must be fought hard. However, other fires should be allowed to burn as part of the natural cycle. And, says Halter, in some cases we should be developing a policy of induced burns. They would mimic the natural process in managed forests and restore the natural process to wild forests in protected areas.

If humans fail to incorporate fire into their forest management equations, he suggests, nature may increasingly do it for them. The terrifying spectacle of BC's recent summer infernos may become the commonplace, as they have in Australia and California, rather than the exception.

Halter has argued that there is preliminary evidence that BC is gradually warming as a consequence of global climate change and that precipitation during summer months is diminishing. This, coupled with the fuel increase caused by a rapid spread of tree-killing insects, simply compounds the natural fire risk.

But he suggests that previous fire-suppression policies of governments in Canada and the United States are also key contributors to the hazard.

There's been a spirited debate about whether the best solutions involve logging, controlled burns or debris-laden forests, and indeed, whether aggressive fire suppression by government and industry should even continue. Common sense suggests a combination of the three methods, based on assessments of the risks to humans and other values like aesthetics and commercial interests, offers the most useful solution.

The US federal government has already appropriated $12 billion to be used over the next decade to address the problem of managing what its scientists perceive to be an accelerating fire risk in forest lands.

"Because we have suppressed such natural fires, we have inadvertently created dangerous conditions in both commercial forests—those slated to be logged—and in national and provincial parks," Halter wrote at the height of the 2003 fire season.

"Over the past few decades, natural woodland debris— that is, fallen trees, branches and old undergrowth—have accumulated more densely on the forest floor. Now, when the weather turns dry and a forest fire occurs, that fire becomes bigger than ever, capable of incinerating everything in its path—including rural communities."

That's precisely what happened in 1922 to the community of Merville, a few kilometres south of these beautiful woods on the flood plain of the Oyster River.

The biggest of the old-growth trees had been logged when the land was pre-empted to provide homesteads for soldiers returning from World War I in 1918. The Douglas firs were so big that on average it took a hundred sticks of black powder to blow one stump. These trees had survived the ancient fires mapped by scientists.

Those left standing were commercially undesirable and of a small but mostly uniform size. Around them the slash had been accumulating, and there were large openings left by homesteads and logging. When a hot, dry wind sprang up at noon on July 6, it whistled through the openings in the trees. A fire smouldering in the logging debris awakened. The breeze caught it, and it took off like a racehorse.

Some years ago when I chatted with Stan Hodgins, who was a child in Merville at the time, the events of 1922 were still etched indelibly into his memory.

"Oh, she was a dandy," he said. "The fire would jump half a mile at a time. I can still see them big limbs, big as my arm, tumbling like tumbleweeds, all in flames. It's hard for you to imagine now, but it was pretty terrifying."

Marjorie Lever, also a child at the time, told me that it had been an exceptionally dry summer. "The ferns were so dry you'd touch them and they'd crumble." She'd been out in the garden when what she thought were big maple leaves began dropping softly on the roof like gigantic snowflakes. It was ash. Then came the roar.

"You could see the trees flaring. That was the fire coming, and we were afraid."

After it began crowning through the smaller timber, nothing on earth could have held the Merville fire, concluded the *Comox Argus*. A near-cyclonic wind carried a rolling wall of flaming branches, bark and embers before it and quickly overran fire crews, who simply dropped their tools and fled.

Three of them, a logger named Churchill and two Merville war veterans named Fenwick and Barr, were trapped and took shelter under Black Creek bridge. The wooden structure caught fire. They lay down in the water of the creek to escape the heat as the fire raged overhead. The scorching was so intense that the creek itself began to evaporate, and by the time the fire had abated, the three men were lying in a steaming trickle.

"The wind was terrible," says the entry in Geoffrey Capes's diary for that day. "The roar of the fire behind was deafening and it was nearly pitch dark with smoke."

Families found they had only minutes to evacuate their homes. Most households were in the sole charge of the women, the men having left immediately to fight the fire. They gathered their little children and made a dash for safety.

One mother had her children in the bath, the *Argus* reported. She looked up once and everything was serene. She looked up a moment later and saw the barn burst into flame. She grabbed the babies and fled down a road as the trees on either side exploded.

Those who tried to drive their automobiles down the Island Highway, then little more than a gravel road, found the paint and rubber catching fire. They abandoned the burning vehicles and fled on foot. Courtenay was soon swamped with refugees.

When the homesteaders returned, the whole settlement at Merville had been erased. Many never rebuilt. Some did. But the settlement dispersed. Today it consists of a general store at the crossroads, an RV lot, a roofing supply business and a few still-blackened spars and stumps.

The 1922 fire only foreshadowed what was to come in 1938. What's still known as the Big Fire began with a small blaze in a stack of logs near Campbell River. It was quickly extinguished.

But it hadn't rained since mid-April, and the fire smouldered underground. A week later on July 14, when the wind sprang up, the fire exploded. It jumped Lower Campbell Lake and destroyed Forbes Landing.

Crews set backfires. The fire jumped the firebreaks. As it moved south, it began to crown. Black Creek and Merville, which had been burned sixteen years earlier, were spared this time. But the fire laid waste to the forests in the Oyster River flood plain and threatened the village of Headquarters, the farming settlement at Dove Creek, the coal mining town of Bevan and the cities of Cumberland and Courtenay.

"And the old snags burned like candles on the Devil's birthday cake," Vancouver reporter Torchy Anderson told his enthralled readers as he watched the fire sweep along the skyline of Constitution Hill. Ash from the fire fell as far away as Portland.

Men were conscripted to fight the fire on Depression wages of twenty-five cents a day. The navy dispatched two warships to Comox Harbour to serve as communications headquarters. Seventeen hundred largely untrained fire-fighters were thrown onto the line at a time when there were few logging roads, almost no heavy equipment and no water bombers available.

As at Merville and Kelowna, at Fernie and Kamloops, it was not the fire bosses who eventually stopped the Big Fire—which alone consumed timber sufficient to construct two hundred thousand new homes—it was nature that brought the fires to heel.

The prospect of more such fires as a consequence of changes in precipitation patterns caused by global warming is troubling. Yet the US Department of Energy's Lawrence Berkeley National Laboratory issued a sober warning in 1998 that one result of climate change for the US will be a dramatic increase in the number of severe fire events, a potential doubling of the annual area burned and a rapid escalation in both firefighting and insurance costs and associated economic losses.

Research conducted in southeastern BC for the Canadian Forest Service points out that the US is acting decisively because Americans are convinced that there is a relatively brief window of opportunity—perhaps fifteen to thirty years—for effective, aggressive policy-making before "uncontrollable, catastrophic wildfires become widespread."

If money talks, the US Congress appears to be taking the prospect seriously. But right now, the research paper says, "in BC we are lagging behind in our recognition of the problem and the associated risks we face."

Do federal and provincial governments have the political will to launch the necessary policy debate from which we must shape a strategic solution to the summers of fire that lie in our future?

The question sings out from the lush second growth where a season of destruction similar to our own once swept the forest that the Padre walked in search of personal renewal.

The Final One Percent

The first real winter weather had bedevilled the evening commute with an evil sleet of snow and rain. Overnight, temperatures dropped below freezing. When I rose in the pre-dawn darkness, I had doubts about whether to even try for my meeting in the cold shadow of Mount Arrowsmith, the craggy Vancouver Island peak that broods over the claustrophobic pass between Nanaimo and Port Alberni.

But some days you just get lucky. The cold front moved through, the thermometer nudged up a couple of degrees and instead of black ice I found clear, wet roads, a cloudless sky and the molten amber of a stunning sunrise.

Gary Murdock, a retired forestry technician, Scott Tanner, a property manager who spent six years in municipal politics at Qualicum, and Phil Carson, a local filmmaker, had invited me to see something unique: a remnant of the primeval forest that once covered Vancouver Island's mild cast coast.

So I drove north over the treacherous Malahat, the

mountain ridge that separates the provincial capital at Victoria from the Cowichan Valley, then on past the still logy communities at Duncan, Chemainus and Ladysmith. I dodged Nanaimo's congestion and continued on past Nanoose Bay and Parksville before swinging west, following the course of the Little Qualicum River to its source in the deep, dark waters of Cameron Lake.

I first drove this pass as a kid more than fifty years ago when it was a gravel logging road and loggers hadn't started felling the great Douglas fir stands that once seemed endless. Today, say environmental organizations like the Western Canada Wilderness Committee, careful analysis of satellite photos provides evidence that three-quarters of the ancient forests that once covered Vancouver Island have been logged.

True, about six percent of the island's geography is protected in parks—if you can call it protection when the provincial government permits hydro development, mining and industrial road building within their boundaries and has begun entertaining proposals from private interests to build resorts. But environmentalists point out that 65 percent of this protected area is actually naked rock, ice fields, alpine tundra, bogs or scrub or has already been logged. Of the remaining 35 percent, less than one percent is said to be old-growth Douglas fir forest.

Today, according to the provincial government, a 1995 study estimated that only 0.5 percent—about eleven hundred hectares—of the island's low coastal plain is still occupied by relatively untouched old-growth forest. Put another way, 99.5 percent has now been logged, carved up by roads or degraded by urban and industrial development.

In the Cameron Valley, a tattered remnant of those splendid forests has been preserved in tiny H.R. Macmillan Provincial Park, better known as Cathedral Grove; a sense of the sacred seems to permeate this stand of gigantic trees, some of which may date back to the reign of the first Queen Elizabeth.

We left our truck at a pullout on Highway 4 near Summit Lake and started hiking.

It was midmorning and one of those splendid days you never forget. Ghostly pockets of mist hung in the mountain hollows. The snowfields on Arrowsmith glittered in the sunshine. The air was clean and crisp.

The night's fast-moving storm had left about a foot of fluffy white powder on the ground, and the trees were laden. Everywhere the forest rippled with the thump of snow clumps tumbling from the canopy, frequently down our necks.

We turned down an unused logging road, then took an even less-used spur, following it uphill for a couple of kilometres, then down again until it petered out in the underbrush. Now we continued by easing our way over deadfalls and through tangles of salal.

The trail stopped abruptly. Before us was a precipice. In the slippery conditions, I stayed well back from the edge but close enough to look into the abyss. Far below, maybe the height of a fifty-storey building down, I glimpsed the icy river roaring among a grove of immense trees.

"That's it," Tanner told me. "Cameron River Canyon. Old growth doesn't get any older than that. This is about as pristine as pristine can be."

Then he turned to follow Murdock through a notch in

the rock and down a narrow, barely defined track. Footing was treacherous in the snow, but I managed to traverse the slopes by hanging onto saplings and exposed roots.

After half an hour of climbing, the trail brought us back to the cliff face. We worked our way aslant down the steeply inclined piles of mossy rubble, past cave openings and undercuts until we came to one of the wonders we were looking for.

A massive western yew, its ancient, slow-growing trunk bigger around than my arm span, twisted away from the cliff. Later I'd come back and measure the trunk using my belt—two lengths, plus a couple of buckle widths, plus a hand span. I calculated it at a hair less than 2.7 metres in circumference, which would make it the fourth or fifth largest specimen recorded in the province.

Below it, the river shot between snow-covered bars, the current dark yet clear as glass over the coloured pebbles. It was cold in the deep shadow of the canyon floor. Sunlight penetrated the narrow aperture of the cliffs only in occasional brilliant shafts, sometimes glistening with refracted light over the whitewater chutes.

I pushed on to where the river raced past, working my way down the trunk of a fallen cedar and around the massive tangle of its root ball, then splashing through some shallows and up to a narrow snow-clad flood plain in a bend of the river.

I could see my breath, and only the salal showed through the snow. But in summer, I'd later learn, along its edges where the light could penetrate the canopy, the little glade would be redolent with the scent of wildflowers. The creamy droop of goat's beard, the crimson splash of columbine, the feathery kelly green of new maidenhair ferns, the rich petals of salmonberry blooms, a froth of Indian celery and a pink, perfumed flutter of wild rose would all adorn this austere winter landscape.

Then I stopped and stared at what the three men had brought me to see.

Here some of the biggest red cedars and Douglas fir I've seen soared up toward the thin ribbon of sky. They were huge, magnificent, probably eight hundred and perhaps a thousand years old. Imagine that: trees already growing when Ethelred the Unready was king of England.

I paused and listened to the wind shaking the snow from the branches, the white noise of the river strangely muffled by the forest.

Then my three guides showed me the blue paint and the fluorescent pink marking tape.

"This remnant of the old forest survived because they couldn't get the timber out if they cut it," Murdock told me. "Not any more . . . [now] there's helicopter logging."

Each one of these trees, its life measured in close to a millennium or perhaps more, might make an hour's work for some logger's chainsaw. Were those trees marked for cutting or just for inventory and forest management?

I considered the possibilities and concluded that if less then one percent of this particular ecosystem remains, then there's no moral justification for taking any more of it, whatever the legal rights and economic rationalizations might be.

No, I thought, it isn't right. This insanity—shoot the last elephant, harpoon the last whale, cut the last big tree—that permeates our heedless, wastrel culture has got to stop and it might as well stop here. The tiny surviving fragment of ancient forest in Cameron River Canyon deserves better than to have its eight hundred or a thousand years turned into toilet paper and two-by-fours.

Brass Casings
and Thirty Pieces of Silver

A shimmering, spectral mist hangs over water-polished boulders where Cottonwood Creek seethes and bubbles into stone punchbowls, as though God were pouring his own bottomless glass of champagne.

Around me the vapour condenses on great, moss-covered maples. Here and there against the naked grey underbrush, a spray of green—so vivid it almost hurts the eye—marks the timeless rite of earliest spring bursting into leaf.

It's difficult to think of such a beautiful landscape as a killing ground, where some fear that the Roosevelt elk, one of BC's most magnificent and vulnerable creatures, is threatened by a grim combination of poachers and industrial economics.

Just up from the stream edge, I find evidence that these ancient and immense creatures have been here before me, using the valley bottoms as their highway as they have since time immemorial.

A mature Roosevelt bull can stand almost two metres high at the shoulder, weigh as much as the BC Lions' defensive front four and carry an eight-point rack of antlers that sweep another metre into the sky.

When I kneel to search for tracks I find water has seeped into a pair of teacup-sized crescents in the earth. Beside the hoofprints lies a scattering of smooth, oval pellets about the size of those small, foil-covered Easter eggs. They give off a sweet, vaguely yeasty scent and still radiate a faint warmth, the lingering body heat of the great animals that left them behind. And the water in the tracks is still cloudy; they aren't long gone. But gone they are.

I am spending my Sunday north of Youbou, about sixty kilometres up the Cowichan Valley from Duncan, hoping to spot a herd of ten elk that two hikers told me they'd seen near Cottonwood Creek just after first light.

By the time I walk into the area, however, the shaggy-shouldered, chocolate-brown Roosevelts have faded silently back into the forest like shadowy apparitions. Not that there is much cover left into which they can retreat from unwanted human company.

Intensive logging operations have begun to strip much of the remaining forest habitat where the Cowichan Lake herd takes shelter from predators, winter wind chill and deep snows.

"Yes, as we speak there is a lot of activity on private land [where the herd winters]," acknowledges Doug Janz, a wildlife section head for the BC government based in Nanaimo. "On Crown land we'd be recommending visual screens along [logging] mainlines, we'd be recommending smaller clear-cuts, we'd be recommending [that loggers leave] large blocks for shelter and snow retention."

But private forest land is governed by different rules

than public land, and Janz might as well be whistling down the wind. Big timber companies are now removing critical winter range for this blue-listed species both in the Cottonwood Creek area north of Cowichan Lake and in the Jump Lake region west of Nanaimo.

For a species to qualify for blue listing, a federal committee of expert scientists must consider it vulnerable to possible extirpation from its range. And here we are, supposedly at the dawn of a new age of enlightenment, placing the Roosevelt elk in a more precarious position by further disrupting what remains of crucial habitat throughout the northern extension of its range.

Perhaps thirty-five hundred Roosevelt elk now survive in BC, and this unique subspecies is concentrated on Vancouver Island, though a few have established themselves on the adjacent mainland.

These fascinating ungulates can be dated back to the last ice age and are closely related to the European red deer, with which they can be bred. It's thought they crossed the Bering land bridge to North America during the last interglacial period and then flourished here.

Aside from caribou, elk are the only member of the deer family to form large herds. They were among the first to repopulate what's now Canada after the ice sheets retreated.

Eventually they numbered in the millions. European settlers, however, quickly hunted the North American elk population to near-extinction. By 1900 fewer than a hundred thousand animals survived on the continent.

Of the six distinct subspecies of North American elk, two are now extinct, and Canada's Roosevelt population is at serious risk. To make things worse, the descendants of the same heedless fools who almost wiped out the elk the first time around are now back at it. Since the beginning of December, taking advantage of logging roads and clear-cuts where the elk gathcr in the open to feed on easy new browse, poachers have gone through the herd on the north shore of Cowichan Lake like a scythe.

"We know of eighteen [Roosevelt elk] that were killed between early December and the first week of February," Duncan-based conservation officer Gary Horncastle tells me when I call to confirm the appalling stories I heard in Youbou.

"The population of that herd is probably in the neighbourhood of 250. Two pregnant cows were shot. There were ten elk kills concentrated in one small area."

When I ask, Horncastle corroborates what anyone with common sense already knows: "Clear-cuts and slash create new opportunities for the elk—and new opportunities for the poachers."

How damaging was this slaughter? Janz said it approaches what big-game biologists consider the annual sustainable harvest target for a herd of that size. In other words, many more unexpected mortalities and the population might tip into an irreversible decline.

Mike Stini, an ungulate specialist who works out of Port Alberni, worries equally about the impact of habitat loss to logging.

"This is a problem [for Roosevelt elk] all over Vancouver Island," said Stini. "It's critical wherever it occurs. At Nanaimo Lakes, just above the second lake, there was a big winter elk range, and now it's just all gone.

"If animals don't have habitat, they can't sustain the

numbers required to maintain healthy populations. But the [forest] companies don't seem to recognize this habitat when it's on private land. They feel the Crown land provides sufficient habitat."

What we are doing to the Roosevelt elk, we are doing to our own dreams.

Heedlessly, hands held out for our thirty pieces of silver, we permit the dismantling of a noble conservation legacy. It was the vision for which brave souls like Roderick Haig-Brown, Ian McTaggart-Cowan, Cowichan elders, the nameless volunteers of the BC Wildlife Federation and other environmental groups have all fought, never yielding in their belief that we might yet salvage something of this province's natural splendour for the generations to come.

A Lament from Crying Girl Prairie

Pat Brady met me in the bush where a muddy track petered out west of Mile 143 on the Alaska Highway, his coal black hair barely flecked with silver despite his sixty-eight years, almost all of them spent as a trapper, horse wrangler, rodeo rider, rancher and outfitter.

His saddle horses were tethered to a clump of trembling aspen, dark shadows against the silvery white trunks upstream from where Cypress Creek sings toward its confluence with the Halfway River. Droplets from a dawn rain still sparkled on the tips of leaves, and the long grass blades drooped beneath their burden.

We walked the horses for a while to limber them up, scratching their ears and talking to them by way of introduction. Then I swung into the well-worn saddle on the mustang that Brady had caught wild and broken for riding here in the beautiful, biologically diverse, almost miraculous landscape of the northern Rockies that sprawls more than a thousand kilometres north of Vancouver. Some have likened it to African savannah for its sheer abundance of large wildlife.

Free-ranging herds of bison, caribou, Stone sheep, moose, grizzly and black bear, deer and elk, timber wolves, lynx and wolverine, all populate a wilderness that can only be accessed on foot or horseback or by floatplane or heli-copter. The region is an echo from the human origins of what's now British Columbia. A similar terrain must have greeted those first ice age hunters coming into a new contin-ent from the cold, arid tundra of Beringia, the land bridge that connected North America to Asia and funnelled new-comers down an ice-free corridor along these same Rocky Mountains perhaps twenty thousand years earlier.

The present boreal forest and the ecosystems that sus-tain and are sustained by all these creatures wouldn't estab-lish themselves for another ten thousand years or so, but evidence of the earliest human occupation in what's now Canada's westernmost province was found not far from here at Charlie Lake near Fort St. John. There, digging in 1983 and again in the early 1990s, archeologists found stone points and animal remains, including what appear to be butchered bison and the bones of snowshoe hares, jack-rabbits and ground squirrels, which date from about 10,500 years ago. The site is matched by another at Vermilion Lakes near Banff, where artifacts and animal remains have been dated to roughly the same period.

Our breath, horse and human, mingled on the crisp morning air. The mustang's coat was still shaggy from a late northern spring, and I was grateful for the animal's warmth. I turned the wiry little buckskin and followed Brady through a narrow parting in the trees to begin our poignant journey deep into the province's past.

Just over a hundred years ago—a minuscule blink in

time by comparison to the tenure of those Neolithic hunters whose descendants still occupy the landscape—thirty-two men and sixty horses of the North West Mounted Police left Fort Saskatchewan near Edmonton. Their daunting mission was to cut a trail through the largely uncharted wilderness from Fort St. John near the Alberta border all the way to Whitehorse in the Yukon.

This amazing Canadian precursor to the Alaska Highway, a wartime project that required ten thousand US Army Engineers and six thousand civilians, was planned when gold was discovered in the Klondike in 1897. Greedy Edmonton merchants had promoted a route that eliminated passage through Skagway, Alaska, where Soapy Smith's thugs and gangsters preyed on the hapless, and then over the brutal Chilkoot and White passes.

The supposedly safer route was a marketing scam. Luckless prospectors who followed the Edmonton scheme encountered only tangles of deadfalls, quaking bogs, bloodsucking insects, starvation and frequently an unmarked grave. A year and a half later, survivors began stumbling into Telegraph Creek on the lower Stikine River.

The condition of the disabled and dying was so shocking the BC government rushed to open a hospital for them in the tiny Tahltan Indian settlement.

Ottawa ordered the Mounties to survey the route and clear a way for pack trains to the goldfields. Between 1905 and 1907, the NWMP blazed a trail that pushed more than 450 kilometres to a point about 125 kilometres north of New Hazelton.

The trail was marked with mileposts, and a log cabin was built every fifty kilometres or so. One of the cabins along the police trail was built in 1905 by Brady's father, Baxter Brady, who had been a fur trader, packer, trapper and rancher long before the prospectors, Mounties and farmers arrived. Pat Brady himself used the cabin while trapping more than fifty years ago. And for many years now Brady has been clearing deadfalls from the old NWMP trail, putting up new mileposts where the old ones have rotted and then bringing people out on horseback to experience the province's remarkable legacy.

"In the old days, this was all packed right down," Brady said as we threaded our way through the trees that crowded the narrow trail and I worked to keep my horse from stopping to browse. "It got a lot of use. There were packers through here all the time. I was young then. I was a wrangler for McCusker."

He must have been some cowboy. When he wasn't wrangling, breaking horses and leading pack trains, Brady made enough money riding saddle broncs on the rodeo circuit to eventually buy his own ranch.

As we rode, the sure-footed mountain mustang picking its way down steep slopes and across creeks, Brady pointed out old mileposts buried in moss, a bundle of teepee poles left by some long-forgotten First Nations family, bits of packers' gear abandoned beside the trail, crushed grass where a moose calf had rested and the shredded bark where a bear had recently stripped a tree to get at the sweet sap.

We crossed countless game trails, pausing to look at wolf tracks and bear scat. Up ahead, Brady told me, was a buffalo jump where hunters stampeded bison. One foggy winter day the approach was icy, and three people went over the cliff with their prey.

"When I was a kid, I found some old spearheads there. And bones," Brady mused. His tale made me think again of Charlie Lake.

He led me through a meadow where wildflowers grew belly-high, pointing to ancient native Indian burial mounds and the white crosses he'd put up himself so less discerning travellers might recognize the place.

Who was buried there? Brady said that long ago he'd asked an elder—"a guy with a lot of power, eh, lot of power"—only to be told the graves were none of his business, and that he really didn't want to know the details. Perhaps it was something like Crying Girl Prairie, south of us on the Graham River, where an epidemic obliterated a native Indian band in the early years of the twentieth century, leaving only a single survivor, whose grief endures in the place name. Maybe it was something more sinister, violence from an even earlier time. Does anyone now remember what happened here? Does it matter? Or is the question merely the idle curiosity of an information magpie?

When we stopped at his father's old cabin, the roof fallen in and the stove rusting out, he reminisced about the time he'd set down a can of fruit on the stovetop and forgotten it—"a couple of young guys, eh"—and then got jammed in the tiny doorway with his partner, both of them trying to get out after it exploded with an awful bang.

I asked Brady what ingredients went into the hot, fragrant mug of "bush tea" he'd brewed for us and to which he attributes his youthfulness. He waved an expansive hand across the ground cover, leaves, shrubs and trees. "Everything," he said. "Everything I need is right here."

Then he took me to look at what was really on his mind.

Orange logger's tape marked "skid road." Timber cruisers' numbers painted on old-growth trees so close to the trail I could lean out and touch them from my saddle. Skidder tracks hacked across the trail that he'd so painstakingly restored and then left like eroding wounds in the earth itself.

"They have no respect," Brady said, leaning on his saddle horn. "They have no respect for the rivers. They have no respect for any of this. I don't have any respect for them."

"We're in the south end of the Muskwa-Kechika," he said. "They even got a nice big sign over there." He gestured toward a distant fringe of trees.

The Muskwa-Kechika is the special management zone spanning the northern Rockies where successive provincial governments have earnestly promised to preserve and protect the astonishingly rich wildlife, habitat and scenic values. It includes a series of major parks, ecological reserves and protected areas for sensitive landscapes. The management zone was carefully designated not to infringe upon and to accommodate the values, interests and needs of First Nations in the region. But with global demand driving up commodity prices, there's increased pressure for access to the remote region for logging, mining, drilling and wellheads, the necessary infrastructure of roads, pipelines and pumping stations and the attendant problems of waste disposal and pollution. Tensions between industry and its supporters in government and other traditional users of the land—farmers, First Nations, guides and outfitters—have been running high across BC's northeast, with lawsuits and protests, some legal and some not.

Brady says he's concerned about the impact on wild game of clear-cutting in this small corner of what many biologists call North America's Serengeti. He's also troubled about the future health of Cypress Creek, since cutting is planned all over its extensive flood plain. Erosion and sedimentation is one worry. Another is industrial pollution. Indeed, Brady directed me to one pile of logging debris near the trail where I found an enormous puddle of what appeared to be some kind of transmission or engine oil still soaking into the ground.

"There's a spring here that runs into Cypress. That's going to get polluted," said Brady. "I think that water should be analysed."

But what angers him the most is the prevalent attitude toward the historic NWMP Trail, where the province has allocated timber cutting rights on Crown land. He says the logging company appears to interpret that as meaning it can clear-cut right up to the trail, utterly destroying its visual and cultural context. Not that those who know the price of every stick of timber and the value of nothing else are likely to pay much attention to an old rancher philosophizing about the importance of our collective cultural heritage.

Yet we'd do well to listen. What I saw on parts of Brady's hand-cleared section of the NWMP Trail looked a lot like the desecration of heritage had already begun, one man's single-handed work to preserve a dramatic piece of our irreplaceable heritage being vandalized in the name of the almighty dollar with his government's bland and blind approval.

Magic at Myra Canyon

Exactly twenty kilometres southeast of Okanagan Mission, beyond the hair-raising switchbacks of an old stagecoach trail, stands what I whimsically like to call the sixteenth wonder of the world.

It's not the pyramids, exactly, and it's partly a work of the imagination now, the originals having been destroyed in a disastrous forest fire in 2003, but as far as frontier engineering goes, it's close. I first experienced it as a kid in the late 1950s, more interested in putting pennies on the track for passing trains to flatten, largely oblivious to its significance—until I returned to look at it with a new appreciation in 1990, never imagining it would vanish into smoke and ash.

To get there, visitors must follow a road that snakes up from the arid Okanagan Valley floor, climbing about a kilometre up to the snowline and beyond. There visitors get a first-hand look at the scale of Mother Nature's engineering and what it imposes on the puny humans who must deal with it. The magnitude of the natural scale is precisely what makes the small human endeavour I first came to see so impressive.

Off to the south rises the high, rocky citadel of Little White and, beyond it, Nipple Mountain and China Butte, all part of the immense volcanic arcs created along the crumple zone where North America slammed into the Pacific Plate about two hundred million years ago.

Little White's name is a kind of sly joke on Big White, Kelowna's famed skiing destination, which lies to the east and has precisely two hundred metres more of altitude. Somehow, I think, these stacked accretionary wedges and jumbled blocks of basalt that comprise much of the Little White country—and which remain unchanged by the ravages of fire, climate change and forest cover—will never really appeal to the downhill crowd's collective aesthetic.

Yet it wasn't the collision of continental plates and the subsequent eruptions, magma flows and tephra—as geologists call the rock ejected from volcanoes—that most visibly marked the present landscape. It was moving water, both liquid and solid: first the huge weight of glaciers two kilometres thick, then the scouring of silt-laden torrents as the ice began its increasingly rapid retreat more than ten thousand years ago.

Man's marks are minuscule by comparison. On the way up, signs peppered the roadside. Nailed to larches and jack pines that crowded the track, they warned of impending doom from logging trucks bound down from the high country to the valley log sorts. The logging trucks weren't what worried me. I had checked the day's traffic schedule before setting out.

What was scary was the way the road surface slicked

out under an unpleasant mixture of snow and freezing rain. I was halfway up and I was already worried about getting back down in my agile, powerful Jeep. I knew I wouldn't want to pilot a fully loaded logging truck down these grades in these conditions. I had become a convert to four-wheel drive one nasty winter long ago; now I was driving a Jeep for just this kind of back-road conundrum. Yet even four-by-fours will skate off the road in really greasy conditions.

Far below the steep drops from the road ran the white water of Klo Creek, tumbling toward its confluence with Hydraulic Creek, itself a tributary of Mission Creek, a major water source that empties into distant Okanagan Lake at the estuary where people have been claiming to see Ogopogo since the turn of the century.

At the foot of these mountains are vast talus slopes; rock pieces shatter off the faces during the seasonal exchanges between summer heat and winter ice.

This day, flurries of snowflakes punctuated the brilliant shafts of sunlight that burst out of a turbulent sky and strode across the highlands like beams from alien spacecraft in some science fiction movie. Deep in the gloomy canyon, I witnessed a spectacle that no Hollywood special-effects team could ever match. Lashed by the sudden, swirling wind, the last sheltered drifts of aspen and poplar were paying tribute to the arrival of winter by snowing torrents of gold leaf across the black rock.

At the top of the tormented track, I came to an intersection.

Straight and level as an arrow, the railbed of the Kettle Valley Line still sweeps from north to south, the longest

2.2-percent grade on the continent. It's a perfect statement on the skills of its Edwardian engineers who built it through some of railroading's most demanding terrain between 1910 and 1916.

Planned and constructed to prevent the monopolization of freight to and from the booming mining camps—spawned by the silver discoveries in the East Kootenay region in the late nineteenth century—the Kettle Valley Line provided an alternate route to tidewater at Vancouver. It also inadvertently charted the route through the Coquihalla Pass that would later become a major highway link between the West Coast and the Interior.

As trucks displaced trains in the movement of freight, improved highway routes through the Crowsnest, Rogers and Yellowhead passes amplified their impact. Secondary rail lines like the Kettle Valley increasingly fell into disuse. By the early 1960s sections of the railway were being abandoned, and it was last used in 1964.

By the time I returned as a curious observer, the steel had long since been pulled and the ties torn up, but the railbed remained as true as it was when Andrew McCulloch's navvies drove the last spike on this section of the railway above Kelowna in 1914.

To see his work, I had to pick my way around a washout where a trestle has collapsed, avoiding the sinkholes and rock slides of neglect. From there I headed south, somewhat nervously, as my Jeep shuddered and shimmied across the ties of first one age-blackened trestle, then another.

On one side the cliff crowded the railway bridge. On the other, inches away, a sheer drop fell away into the canyon—a height greater than the tallest building in Vancouver.

When a rockfall blocked a tunnel that had been blasted through the cliff, I abandoned my Jeep and hiked on through the rubble. At the far entrance, hunched into my jacket against a wind that cut like John Masefield's proverbial "whetted knife," I looked out on the awesome vista of Myra Canyon.

To conquer it, McCulloch's construction crews spanned eighteen chutes, canyons, and precipices in one seventy-kilometre span of track. Sixteen of the trestle sites were simultaneously visible from where I stood. Is there anything to match the magic of this panorama in railway engineering history? To be sure, there are long trestles and high trestles, roundhouses and amazing tunnels, but is there anything to match the sixteen trestles crowded into this brutal, unforgiving terrain?

This stretch of railway was once renowned as the most remarkable in the world—a living symbol of Canada's pioneering genius. It reveals a technical brilliance so spectacular it resembles art as much as engineering technology.

Then, in the early morning hours of August 16, 2003, a lightning bolt struck a snag somewhere near Squally Point, where Okanagan Lake doglegs north toward Kelowna. Whipped by strong winds, the fire raced through tinder-dry stands of pine. It eventually destroyed more than two hundred homes on the outskirts of the Okanagan Valley's largest city, which has a metropolitan population of more than 160,000. Among the casualties were twelve of McCulloch's amazing wooden railway trestles.

But with support from various levels of government and volunteer organizations, the burned trestles were reconstructed, and the magic at Myra Canyon was reborn as a popular trail and backcountry bicycle route in 2008. This homage to the value of British Columbia's history was as admirable, in its own small way, as the building of McCulloch's Kettle Valley Railway was in the first place.

The Old Man and the River

With a sibilant green hiss, one of Canada's most renowned trout rivers slithers eastward over smooth brown bottom pebbles. Here and there, surface boils signal a hole or boulder deep beneath the swift, froth-laced current while swollen back eddies suck greedily at banks clad with dense tangles of tree roots and overhanging willow branches.

It's a gloomy winter morning on the stretch of the upper Cowichan long-known to anglers as Willow Run. Snow still lingers in shady nooks. Above us distant peaks like Waterloo and Whymper soar a kilometre into the sky, gleaming in their white mantle of wind-sculpted drifts and cornices—if only one could see them.

For now a cold, dank mist hangs in the treetops and a steady bone-chilling drizzle of rain has begun to dimple the surface, dripping off the brim of my hat, trickling down my neck and making the inside of my ancient Mustang floater coat as clammy as the bottom of a rubber raft.

Behind me fishing guide Joe Saysell leans on his oars,

deftly catches the outside curl of one of those big eddies and sideslips his flat-bottomed skiff just along the edge of a gravel bar where the water begins to shallow.

This drift boat, built to a design developed for maximum safety on the turbulent, fast-flowing, rock-filled rivers of Oregon, draws only a few centimetres of water, yet the high prow where I sit wedged into a notched seat gives me a clear view through the surface reflections, rippling shadows and light distortions cast by the racing current.

I'm looking for big, slab-sided winter-run steelhead, which are the huge, seagoing rainbow trout for which this river became famous with serious sports anglers around the world. There should be a score of them lying like dark bars of iron beneath the current, waiting to deposit the eggs of a new generation in the bottom gravel.

But there are none.

There are plenty of trout, some as long as my forearm, but not one steelhead. Joe shakes his head in dismay, a spray of rain flying from the brim of his baseball hat to splatter against my coat.

"This half mile is the most productive stretch of the Cowichan," he says.

"Everything spawns here. Trout. Salmon. Look, that's a major steelhead lie over there"— he points to a tawny bar submerged close to the dishevelled bank where willow branches bob and shudder in the tug of the passing water— "I used to see at least a dozen spawners on that bar. There's not a fish."

Joe was born in the Cowichan Valley. He has spent more than sixty years with this stunningly beautiful river. The small house where he and his wife Gail live is right on the banks of this superb trout water, once as famous in London and New York as Isaak Walton's chalk streams and the whiskey-coloured rivers of Ireland.

He's a professional fly-fishing guide with a clientele that comes back year after year, although he notices that as they grow older, they seem less inclined to fish and more inclined to savour the river for its wild beauty alone.

Still, the Cowichan's mystique is such that anglers continue to come from around the world to fish the quick, slashing runs and languid pools for brown trout, rainbows, cutthroat, and of course, for the wary and elusive winter steelhead that remain the true test of anyone who fishes with the fly.

But like most of the overfished streams on the east coast of Vancouver Island, their hydrology changed for centuries to come by logging operations that strip the upper watersheds, the once-great Cowichan and its steelhead runs are in deep trouble.

Which is why, in the summer, when most folks are kicking back with a beer and contemplating the evening barbecue, Joe dons cumbersome rubber waders every day or so, picks up a five-gallon bucket and clumps off down Willow Run.

It's an arduous slog for an aging man troubled by arthritis, up to twelve kilometres through the pools and riffles of the river that has been central to most of his well-lived lifetime. As he walks, Saysell looks for puddles and shallows where baby salmon and trout have been stranded by water levels that dwindle as consecutive summers of drought drag on. As temperature in sun-baked shallows rises, fry die quickly in the stagnant, oxygen-starved water.

Those that do hang on make easy pickings for predators. So every awkward expedition is marked by a sense of urgency.

When he finds stranded fry—and he finds thousands—Saysell scoops them into his bucket and carries them to the river's main stem where they'll at least have a chance to survive. But only a chance, he points out, because as water levels continue to fall, temperatures rise in the main stream too.

"Nobody is talking about water temperature," Saysell says. "But that's what scares me. During summer hot spells, the river's temperature often rises to more than twenty degrees. Can the resident trout withstand that? Can the fry that I'm releasing into the river? If the water flow stays at this height—and that would be optimistic—and if the overall temperature stays at this level, I think you are going to see water temperatures of twenty-four degrees. Then you are going to see fish kills."

Saysell says he recognized the gravity of the situation while he was guiding a client in his drift boat and heard a flock of birds making an unusual commotion. Off behind a gravel bar, right where the birds were making a ruckus, he saw a silvery glint and went to have a look. A puddle left by the falling river was seething with stranded fry.

"I've never seen anything like it," he says. "It was like an enormous herring ball or something."

Around the puddle, the ground was silver with newly dead fish. The woman he was guiding became distraught.

"I thought she was going to cry," he says. "I got my bucket and started scooping the live ones up and carrying them to the river. I took eight buckets out of that one puddle. I estimate there were twenty-five thousand to thirty thousand fish."

From that day Saysell began a regular daily scouting mission, rising early and drifting the river in his boat looking for trapped fish. When the river eventually became too low for his boat, he put on his waders and started walking.

He is quick to point out that he's not alone in this rescue mission. Folks from the Cowichan Tribes and other community-spirited people also walk the river and its tributary creeks to check its adjacent wetlands, the back channels and the streams that empty into Cowichan Lake where the river rises. He estimates that collectively they've so far rescued about a quarter of a million immature trout and salmon.

"These are all wild fish," he says. "We should be salvaging fry like this on the whole coast. Talk about an ideal job for university students for the summer. We could do this everywhere and spend about a tenth of the money we spend on hatcheries."

Saysell brings to his crusade a unique passion that is animated by a lifetime's knowledge of the river he knows as well as the back of his hand.

He's been warning politicians and just about anybody who will listen that a crisis has descended upon the trout and steelhead river than once attracted the world's elite anglers.

They came to fish year-round for brown trout, rainbows and cutthroat; for coho salmon in the late fall; for a run of massive midwinter steelhead and for spring salmon of even greater size that began moving up the river as early as April.

Once the Cowichan was a favourite of the Prince of Wales.

That was then.

Today the watershed is ravaged by logging, fish habitat is squeezed by development and the summer flow is allocated to human uses that claim priority over mere fish.

Joe thinks the priorities are backward, not because he's a fishing guide but because common sense says if the river is able to support an abundant fish population, then it will also be able to support the rest of us.

"If there isn't enough water in the river to support even the fish," he points out, "how is there going to be enough to support us?"

It's a fair point. Once-abundant fish populations have already been seriously depleted. If the diminished remnants are now threatened by insufficient water, how can humans in much greater numbers with much bigger demands expect otherwise?

"It's bad now," Saysell says. "What's going to happen when the population grows as projected and water demand doubles or triples?"

The cause is complex, he agrees. It's occurred at the intersection of serious drought, too little winter snow and growing demand for industrial and recreational purposes. For example, Saysell says, logging in headwaters leaves the watershed unable to retain runoff, which creates a "yo-yo effect" with water tables.

"It rains, and the river now rises rapidly. Then, when the rain stops, the river falls just as rapidly. This is because of headwaters logging. But as soon as I mention irresponsible logging to politicians, their eyes glaze over. Nobody wants to hear about that."

In the interim, at least, Saysell says there's a simple, effective solution. If a weir already at Lake Cowichan were raised by 0.6 metres, it would store enough winter runoff to keep the river's flow constant for both fish and people during what global warming may turn into a perpetual summer drought.

Unfortunately, he says, some residents with cottages on the lake object that if levels are kept higher they might lose some of the annual expanse of summer beach to which they are accustomed.

Saysell says provincial studies fifteen years earlier, right after one of the heaviest winter snows in memory, show those fears to be largely unfounded. In the few cases where property owners might be affected, he thinks the cost of provincial compensation would be far outweighed by benefits to the river and those that rely upon it, both humans and fish.

"Look," Saysell says. "We're in a terrible crisis. We're going to take enormous hits on fish. If water levels get low enough, the pulp mill downstream in Crofton is going to have to close. If the weir gets raised, these guys will have a smaller beach in the summertime. That's the trade-off. I think some people better give their heads a shake."

An interim progress report issued by the Ministry of Environment's Vancouver Island steelhead recovery plan is blunt. Steelhead counts in the Cowichan for 2001–02 had dwindled to less than five fish per kilometre.

On the formal scale set out by the ministry's fish

scientists, the world-famous Cowichan now ranks somewhere between a Level One and a Level Two river for steelhead abundance. Level One is defined as a river in which "fish are rare and at high risk of extinction." Level Two is one where "fish are scarce and at moderate risk."

This is why I'm out with Joe on this miserable morning. We are looking for spawning pairs of steelhead along the bars and in the back eddies where they prefer to lie up, either waiting to spawn or gathering strength for their return to the ocean.

"The Cowichan is our premier river," Joe says as he backs us into the current, which sweeps us away downstream past the pools with their idiosyncratic names: Blasted Rock, Sleepy Hollow, Big Band, Cougar Run, Spring Hole and the Sawdust Pile.

"This is our blue-ribbon trout river, and yet our steelhead run is just a remnant of what it once was. They say the Cowichan is good, but they are comparing it to rivers where there's now almost nothing."

Indeed, just a few months before my expedition with Saysell, the provincial government had imposed total sport fishing closures on thirteen Vancouver Island rivers where steelhead stocks were deemed at risk. Partial closures were imposed on seven more. But the Cowichan, where steelhead are deemed at moderate to high risk, remained open, subject to gear restrictions in a small stretch of the upper river.

And that's what Joe wants to talk about when we beach on a sandbar, light a fire to drive off some of the chill and squat among the wolf tracks to drink hot tea under the gaze of nine bald eagles.

He tells me he wants to see the river above Skutz Falls—the stretch where we've been counting scarce steelhead—restricted to fly-fishing only. Because the river is in winter spate with a strong, very cold current, even the best anglers can't get their flies close to the bottom where endangered fish lie.

But on 85 percent of the Cowichan, anglers are still permitted to use mechanical spinning tackle and external weights that take their lures right down to the steelhead with lethal efficiency.

"For every clean fish they catch, they take ten dark spawners," he points out. And if the spawning fish are released, they can be caught again, sometimes numerous times over several days. Even if the mortality rate for released fish is only 10 percent, he wonders, is that something these beleaguered stocks can sustain? Or should sustain?

Extending the fly-fishing-only zone over the prime steelhead spawning areas above Skutz Falls would deprive gear anglers of access to only 12 percent of the total river—leaving them access to almost 75 percent—Joe says. But it would yield an enormous return in conservation benefits.

Furthermore, he'd like to see a province-wide recreational bag limit of two fish of any species, which he says would go a long way to reducing recreational fishing pressure on the resource.

"This is not rocket science," Joe says. "We have to address this pioneer, buffalo-hunting mentality that thinks the resource is endless. We have to realize that sport fishing isn't just about killing fish, it isn't even necessarily about catching fish. It's about getting out on the river and engaging with nature on the river's terms."

When we beach just above the thundering white chute of Skutz Falls, I leaf through my notebook. In the four-hour drift down the Cowichan, I've counted seven steelhead. One more than the number of anglers I've counted relentlessly working the bottom with their spinning tackle.

Under Blackface Mountain

Above the burying ground, naked slopes sweep up and away to the rough-and-tumble wilderness where Restless River drains north to the Arctic.

The wind is a powerful voice here, shouting the clouds into streamers around peaks with names like Gargoyle Mountain, The Rajah and Llysfran—Raven's Palace in the ancient language of Welsh kings.

But it is this small cemetery that speaks loudest in the huge silence of the Rockies.

I was drawn to it by the bone-white glimpse of something in the ground cover. It flashed in the wan light somewhat less than two kilometres above sea level.

At first there seemed only a handful of graves, then I saw more hidden by strangling vines. Most of the graves are tiny, a size for children. Farther up, a few modest marble slabs are laid down in the willow and bearberry. One wooden marker gleams as if the paint were new, its inscription badly lettered and simple: Annie MacLeod and Son. b. 1899 d. 1927.

Most of these graves are nameless. Identities have been obliterated by time and weather from the simple wooden crosses that tilt and stagger over rough ground.

This is a graveyard of poor people, working people, people who hoarded scraps from the fire to make markers for their children's graves.

People erased from history.

Once the cold, thin air of this valley rang with the enterprise of Mountain Park, a coal town built for investors from Europe's ruling class.

Col. Sir Harold P. Mitchell, descendant of Scottish coal barons, had long been chairman of the Luscar group of companies operating mines in Canada and elsewhere. He was prominent enough to serve as vice-chairman of the British Conservative party under Sir Winston Churchill.

I'd first heard about Mountain Park from documentary filmmaker Tom Radford, who heard about it as a boy from his pioneer grandfather. He recollects, as a young man, mingling at a cocktail party with those who start industries and stop them.

"I heard them talking about the interesting things that investment capital allowed one to do," he said. "And then one of them said something that chilled itself into my memory forever.

"He said: 'Best of all, it lets you own people.'"

Mountain Park was one of those places. A company town with a company store. A company train. Company debts.

More than sixty years ago, when oil displaced coal, the mine closed overnight, with final deductions from the pay stubs to settle outstanding debts. The people were cleared off the site and all the buildings razed. Today slag heaps remain. Even they are largely reclaimed by nature.

But down in the softer foothills, over coffee at the Hole-in-the-Wall store, old-timers told me of the woman who came back year after year.

She came from somewhere a long way away, somewhere in the States maybe.

She'd make her way in from Cadomin, up the road that challenged my Jeep, through the cuts where the huge seams are exposed.

She'd keep on, high above the abandoned railway, passing the washed-out bridge where the rails still hang, held together by ties, screeching as they flail crazily in the wind.

Up here in this stark and beautiful valley, following contours mapped into her brain alone, she'd pace off the foundations of the little houses, each of them twenty-eight feet by twenty-eight feet.

She'd stop where the front doors used to be and speak the names of families long gone. An ancient ritual for human beings; naming the thing makes it real.

Until one year she didn't come. Got tired or died maybe. And the names of the departed disappeared from history like the children they left in the cemetery, like Annie and her son.

The Colonel died in 1983 after an illustrious career. He'd owned plantations in Jamaica, Guatemala, Brazil, Honduras and Fiji and coal mines in Canada and the US. He held honourary degrees—and real ones from Oxford. A brilliant industrialist, it's said.

When he died, the government named a summit after the great man.

Sir Harry Mitchell's mountain isn't visible from the graveyard of the nameless in the town that isn't there.

Blackface Mountain is.

Blackface, as the men were at the end of every bone-weary day of their short working lives. The lives they spent with wives like Annie, building Canada for children who never grew to share it, building fortunes for people who never knew their names or cared.

The Hermit of the Rivers

As the overnight rain eased into a drizzly, half-hearted morning over Campbell River, I made my way toward St. Patrick's Roman Catholic Church for the mass celebrating the forty years since Father Charles Brandt was ordained a hermit priest.

At first Brandt can seem a bit austere, as one might expect of somebody in his eighties who has committed a life to the discipline of an ascetic's regimen of prayer, meditation and self-imposed solitude.

In fact he's a warm, welcoming man, a man of eloquence and imagination, a man of letters. Many people must feel the same way I do, because when I arrived at St. Patrick's, the distractions of Super Bowl Sunday notwithstanding, it was standing room only with Bishop Richard Gagnon of the Diocese of Vancouver Island presiding.

This didn't surprise me, considering the esteem in which Brandt is held, both for the guidance his calm presence offers and for his steady commitment to reconciling the natural world with human affairs both temporal and spiritual.

For Catholics, of course, the rite had a profound religious significance. Brandt represents an ancient tradition of wise men and women withdrawing from the world, the better to reflect upon how best to serve God. Yet I spotted more than a few irreligious folk, even the odd avowed atheist, who had come to honour him too. Can there be higher praise for a holy man than that even unbelievers express gratitude?

Brandt commands respect not only because, as the bishop reminded those present, the hermit's life shows us the importance of silence in a noisy world, but also because of the bigness of his vision. Humanity and nature, Brandt teaches, are braided into a continuity of being and divine purpose that makes them essential to one another.

Among the few officially recognized hermit priests in the western world—he's one of the first to be so ordained in the last two hundred years—Brandt began his contemplative life on the banks of the Tsolum River near Courtenay among a colony of similarly inclined souls who were encouraged by then Bishop Remi de Roo in 1964.

Brandt had served as a navigator with the US Air Force from 1943 to 1946. After the war he did a degree in biology, was ordained as an Anglican priest in 1951, then became a Roman Catholic and eventually emigrated to British Columbia.

The hermitage, just west of the old World War I soldiers' settlement of Merville in the Comox Valley, began with eight men and then grew to thirteen, each required to build his own shelter and provide his own living.

Brandt's chosen profession in the temporal world was to become skilled in the restoration of old and rare books. He committed himself not just to the continued transmission of knowledge but also to its aesthetic, a sensibility that earned him an international reputation as one able to provide salvation to damaged and decaying texts from an age when the book itself seemed a minor miracle.

When the colony later dispersed, Brandt moved to the Oyster River, a bit farther north, which is how I came to know him.

The Oyster is a beautiful stream that rises between Mount Albert Edward and Alexandra Peak and tumbles down to the Strait of Georgia a bit north of Miracle Beach Provincial Park. It's always been renowned for its winter steelhead, cutthroat trout in the lower river and an abundance of pink salmon that can be caught on the fly in the estuary in late July and August.

But the river has taken a drubbing from progress.

Landowners who built on the flood plain sought to tame its meandering with rip-rap that speeded the flow and changed the hydrology. A marina was permitted to gouge a boat basin in the estuary. Loggers moved into the steep slopes and canyons of the upper river, changing runoff patterns.

Where some felt despair, Brandt provided a unifying vision of what might be, advocating the idea of a "sacramental commons" in which all living things, including humans, have their dignity and place.

Around this idea gathered people determined to do better by the little river and each other. Today management of the Oyster River watershed—still not perfect by any means, for what human endeavour can be?—has emerged as a model for co-operative stewardship of a living resource.

That's why I and so many others were quite happy to forego the transient thrills of the professional football circus to honour a tranquil man who meditates upon eternity and whose work is for the ages—starting right now.

Of Snow and Roses

Many of us imagine the geographical centre of Canada to be somewhere in Manitoba. It's not. It's just shy of the Arctic Circle in a treeless desert we call the Barren Ground.

About one-third of Canada is arctic tundra. Most of the rest is either sub-arctic wilderness or feels like it for most of the year. Yet judging from the shock in the media whenever there's a cold snap, you might be forgiven for thinking winter is a surprise visitor to our homeland of kilometre-thick permafrost, glaciers, frozen ocean, ice hockey and most of the world's polar bears.

Well, winter comes, and it comes every year.

One needs neither an almanac nor a thermometer to predict that between Christmas and Palm Sunday, somewhere in this country snow will bury some community and the mercury will plunge to forty below or colder. Actually the mercury won't plunge to forty below because mercury turns solid at minus thirty-eight, but you know what I mean.

Beyond the cozy little toenail of the Fraser River delta

and the southern tip of Vancouver Island, the post-Christmas weather brings three possibilities.

Cold. Colder. D-d-d-damn c-c-c-cold!

On the toenail, the season of good cheer is predictably followed by the season of gloating postscripts. Prairie pals trapped in chilly living rooms with crabby kids (school buses don't run at minus forty) dig out the mailbox to be greeted by reminders that we are strolling the Stanley Park seawall or feeding the ducks in Beacon Hill Park and are simply astounded at how early and abundant the crocuses are this year.

Critical sensibilities here in southwestern British Columbia tend to blur in the same way that the seasons blend into one another. With the great, stark canvas of Canada at our backs, Vancouver sometimes feels like a soft-headed collage of pastels.

I'm not one to assume a smug superiority toward those who must bundle up against blizzards in St. Boniface, howlers in Halifax or chill factors in Chicoutimi.

There is much to love here: the bite of salt and iodine on mild air, the astonishing spectrum of greens that greets a winter visitor descending by plane from the dazzling white of the Interior to the verdant rain forest.

And it's true. Roses bloom in some Victoria gardens in December, a few trees blossom in January and in February snowdrops peep through last year's unraked leaves.

But that's the work of God and El Niño, not of those who happen to live here. Taking personal credit for the gentle West Coast climate and playing the snob over one's good fortune has always seemed a dangerous conceit in earthquake and tsunami country.

Could the smugness in Vancouver and Victoria reflect BC's shrinking sense of frontier patrimony while our self-image as a new Pacific city state inflates? Lotusland once ended at the Rockies. Now, from Fernie to Pouce Coupe, the alienated will remind you with intense urgency that "there's life beyond Hope."

Behind the Coast Range grows a perception that Lower Mainlanders are psychologically decoupling, turning their backs on the historical realities of a province almost as big as western Europe, shrinking the boundaries of Lotusland from the mountain passes to the Fraser Canyon.

Who'd guess, sipping a café society latte outside the library in mild downtown Vancouver, that the third-coldest temperature ever recorded in this country—minus 58.9—was not in Labrador, Arctic Quebec, Nunavut or the Northwest Territories, but here in BC? Or that factoring for wind chill, BC's lowest recorded temperature—minus sixty-nine degrees—is colder than Alberta's?

Who'd guess that the province that brags that at least it doesn't have to shovel the rain has the highest average annual snowfall, triple the average for Ontario and four times the Yukon's average? Or that BC still holds the record for heaviest snowfall in one season, almost twenty-five metres at Mount Revelstoke? Yes, that's metres, not centimetres. Or who would surmise that in any given month, BC has twice as much snow on the ground as any other province or territory?

To be truthful, more than one grey morning I've felt the gloom of the umpty-third day of dank overcast seeping into my spirits. Days like that I think fondly of the clean demarcation of seasons that winter offers so much of our deserted country. There's no doubting the separation of seasons in Fort St. James or Lower Post.

Canada's winter is not just stalled cars, cracked blocks, frozen plumbing and the eternal astonishment of news directors in the self-contained worlds of Toronto, Montreal and Vancouver when they discover, yet again, that the season brings cold weather.

Winter is also the luminous miracle of snow glimmering among birches under a full moon near Kispiox. It's the gritty hiss of snow curling like plumes of smoke across the highway at Kiskatinaw. It's the whiter than white stillness of ptarmigan in the willows. It's the sweet plumes of woodsmoke rising straight to heaven through a star-choked sky above the plain white church at Fort Good Hope.

It's air so cold that when you open your mouth to speak in Dawson City, your words come riding a swirl of ice crystals that glitter as you talk. It's stopping your car in the perfect, pale sunshine near Meadow Lake, Saskatchewan, digging your old CCM skates out of the trunk and sailing away, alone with the wind on a polished slough.

Perhaps we'd all do well to ignore the thoughtless lamentations about cold weather and instead give thanks for winter—even from Vancouver. In a world of changes, the fact that so many of us are born with ice in our blood may be the one defining constant that helps to set our national character.

Godspeed for All the Little Ones

Our golden stretch of days contracts again. The vast machineries of heaven tilt us once more away from the sun and deeper into the cold, timeless shadow of space and the autumnal portents of the winter yet to come.

And yet everywhere the abundance of the earth is evident.

The river shallows seethe with spawning salmon. Raccoons, sleek and sassy, are suddenly picky about what to steal. My last, sweetest tomatoes are coming in. And all across Canada's sun-burnished southwestern quarter, fencelines are heavy with the ripeness of blackberries.

Impenetrable tangles spill over the barbed wire, and kids like mine traverse thorny fringes with empty ice cream pails, mouths and fingers crimson with the juice of berries that will never make it to Mum's jam jars.

The evenings are fragrant and soft, but you look up from dinner on the back deck and notice with surprise that you're already swaddled in black silk and the moon is caught in the gnarled tops of the arbutus and the Garry oaks.

The change of seasons marks, for my wife and me, the end of a bigger phase in the cycle of life.

Our daughter is off to school for the first time, a small thing in the sweep of history, and yet a great rite of passage in thousands of little lives, no less momentous for the thousands of parents for whom it's also a Rubicon.

My own first day at school is buried in my distant, half-forgotten past, but I still remember the one important detail, that tingling instant in which my hand parted from my mother's and I knew instinctively that from then on I was on my own.

I wasn't, of course, and yet I was too, for it's at this precise moment of parting that the child is for the first time formally extracted from the warm comfort of the family cocoon. At home we teach our children the values that prepare them for their own families. At school we civilize them—equip them for the roles they are compelled to take as citizens of the commonwealth.

The warmth and skill and genuine concern of our early childhood teachers notwithstanding, this day is really the first moment of citizenship. It is every new little Canadian's first conscious encounter with the cold impersonality of the state. It is the first time—aside from registering births and vaccinations—that the state intrudes into a new life and says, "We collectively, as a society, have a profound interest in you and in how you turn out as an individual—and we are acting upon that interest."

And quite an interest it is. A multi-billion dollar ticket that consumes about eight percent of every working person's income.

So for little Heledd, although she doesn't comprehend

the magnitude of what's transpired, the first day of school marks the end of childhood's perfect innocence and freedom and the beginning of responsibility.

I don't mean to imply that childhood ends with school. There's plenty of childhood left: too much, perhaps, if you're a child yearning to grow up; not enough if you're a parent who treasures the opportunity to see the world again through eyes unclouded by prejudice, assumptions, stereotypes, all the psychological equipment we invent to automate our perceptions.

But crossing the boundary that separates preschoolers from school kids means leaving behind a world that can never be regained, a world in most cases encompassed entirely by the loving geography of the family and the dominion of parents.

We sacrifice this comforting world to achieve the birth of a new and bigger and more dangerous one.

I got up before dawn and went to watch our daughter sleep. Last night I couldn't get her to bed. Excited at the morning's prospect, she ran on adrenalin until she crashed.

I thought about how suddenly the horizons of a small world are peeled back, and the long trek toward making her own life—and making her own way in that life—begins anew, as it does every year at this time for so many children.

As for her two parents, we've been luckier than some, with interesting, flexible jobs as writers that permitted us to work from home and thus spend most of those first, irreplaceable five years with her.

For they were wondrous years, the years of everything fresh and everything exciting. In her capacity to marvel at and personify the simple things we'd conditioned ourselves to take for granted, we rediscovered our own capacity for wonder.

The awesome discovery of tiny crabs in tide pools and noisy squirrels in Stanley Park, grandmother halibut with both eyes on the same side of her face at the aquarium, flurries of snow geese at the Reifel Bird Sanctuary and that stunned first encounter with North Shore snowflakes.

We all carry fragments of our childhood with us. Among these generalized impressions are the specific events that I know have already lodged in her memory forever: catching her first fish, a five-kilo ling cod as big as she was; Bob the Bear, who grew giddy eating windfalls, climbed into mum's prized Italian apple tree, fell out on his head, and like a bad drunk, chased dad into the house. Sammy the Seal, saved from the killer whales and serenaded all the way to the aquarium—the car still smells of him. Miss Silly Pants, the deer who started as a spotted fawn wagging her shaggy backside and refusing to surrender the road. She survived to bring her twins to eat the geraniums.

This moment too, I expect, will accompany the trajectory of her life, this first separation from the family and the coming at last to the classroom she's desired with all her heart since her friends went off to school.

And for us, the memory of that last, lingering touch of her parents' loving hands, a final apprehensive look backward and then gone into the welcoming embrace and growing whirlwind of what she's longed for.

Godspeed, little one, and all the little ones.

All Things Bring Their Blessings

I called to ask directions from Campbell River, but the voice on the phone sounded thinner than I recalled from past conversations, still courtly, but somehow missing a remembered timbre.

"Keep going past Roddy's house," the voice instructed. That would be the modest house of the late but still esteemed writer, magistrate and university chancellor Roderick Haig-Brown. I knew where that was. I stayed there once during its subsequent reincarnation as a bed and breakfast.

"Look for a sign to your right. It says The Garden of Egan. That's me, but I'm not the gardener anymore."

I found the weathered sign easily enough and turned in on the gravel drive. Van Gorman Egan—fly fisherman, professional guide, retired teacher and fellow writer—greeted me in his book-cluttered study that overlooks the swift Campbell River.

He looked as frail as his voice had sounded, walking a bit uncertainly with a cane, but the words flowed as richly as they ever had.

"I had a stroke back in September 2006," he said, apologetically, as though he might somehow have averted this inconvenience if he'd only known his guest would be coming. "I'll be eighty-two in three months."

And that's why I'd come to see him. All things bring their blessings, and while a stroke is not something I'd wish on anybody, this event had generated its own small miracle in its victim, one that blesses the rest of us.

That fall Egan had been out angling for one of the Campbell River system's mighty Chinook. He was fishing according to the strict rules of the venerable Tyee Club—trolling from a rowboat, single barbless hook, no fish finders, no depth sounders, no powered downriggers, and so on—whose history he published in 1988, having taken honours himself as Tyee Man for landing the largest salmon, a fifty-nine-pounder, the previous year.

The sporting difficulty of the accomplishment is evident in the fact that only a handful of anglers have repeated as winner in the club's eighty-four-year history. Egan himself went almost a quarter of a century between visits to the podium, the first time serving as guide when Richard Fitzpatrick took the honours in 1964.

In 2006 Neil Cameron, editor and publisher of the Campbell River *Courier-Islander*, an old friend and ardent angler himself, was guiding for Egan on the Tyee Pool where the annual derby takes place, when the old fisherman suddenly felt tired and asked to go home.

"We figure he had his stroke out on the Tyee Pool while I was rowing," Cameron said.

He was found at home the next day, slumped in a chair, the left side of his body paralyzed.

That's where the miracle kicked in.

As therapy for the paralysis, Egan was told to start getting his fingers moving in the intricate patterns of typing using the clunky old electric typewriter—clunky only to me, I must add, a scientific wonder to him ("It makes corrections when I make typos!")—on a desk positioned so he can look out across his garden at the racing Campbell River with its fringe of willow and alder.

"I started doing a little typing, just to see how well I could use my left hand," Egan said. "I wrote some of this and some of that. I found that of all the things that my left hand is supposed to do, typing it does pretty well."

Some of this and some of that turned out to be his remembrances of Haig-Brown, his old fishing companion. Slowly the dexterity exercises grew from sentences to paragraphs, then to chapters, and eventually coalesced into a small book. He showed the stories to Cameron. The editor was stunned.

"It's just a beautiful read," said the newspaper guy. "This year is the hundredth anniversary of Haig-Brown's birth, so the *Courier-Islander* decided to publish them in book form as a special commemorative edition."

And so *Shadows of the Western Angler* entered the world, bound in leather and printed on the highest quality paper.

"It has great entertainment value for readers," Cameron said, "but there's also a sense that we have a duty as a local newspaper to make sure this gets recorded for history."

For more than half his life, Egan was a friend and neighbour of Haig-Brown, whose own writings reflected on fish, fishing and the wonders of the natural world and its seasonal cycles on Vancouver Island. More important, he helped shape the foundations of a public conservation ethic that made him an international literary icon.

Egan first met the famous writer in 1954. A farm boy from Wisconsin, he'd read some of Haig-Brown's early writings and travelled west to visit the setting of the books.

"I carried a copy of *The Western Angler*, second edition, and I thought I should get him to autograph it for me. It wasn't the most thoughtful thing to do, I guess, but I just drove in and asked him. He did, of course, and he was very polite about it."

Later that year, after studying the fly patterns recommended in *The Western Angler*, Egan was fishing on the Campbell River. He encountered Haig-Brown again.

"I was up fishing the Sandy Pool and I was using a two-handed rod and figuring out my cast. I didn't know it, but he was up on the bridge watching, He came down onto the sandbar, picked up a Silver Lady fly and said, 'Is this yours?'"

"I reeled in my line and found I was fishing with no fly. I guess it snagged on something, and my leader snapped. But he was pleased that I was using his pattern and he invited me to dinner.

"'Come early,' he said, 'and we'll play croquet.' So I went and played on the lawn and spent a pleasant evening with him and his wife, Anne, in the famous study.

"He later took me fishing up the Elk River before the flooding that came after the dam was built. I'd never had fishing like that in my life.

"It was a pretty river, but it wasn't a beautiful setting. They had logged the valley and pretty well shaved it. Every year you'd have to relearn the river. It would swing from one side of the valley to the other and back. But the trout were there. Everything we caught was cutthroats. Now they seem to take all rainbows. Something is changing."

At the time Egan was running a small motel at Shelter Point, south of Campbell River, and he'd met Maxine, his wife-to-be. She died in November 2005. We paused to look at the photo of her with a forty-eight-pound Tyee, the largest caught by a woman in 1989 and only half a pound larger than the one that won her the same honours in 1964.

Haig-Brown served as best man at the Egans' wedding, and the friendship deepened.

"For a couple of vagabonds, which we were, he was awfully kind to us."

The writer urged Egan to move to Campbell River and take a teaching job. But the teacher's pay was only $2,200 for ten months' work, and with the bills of the newly married coming in, he instead went to tend bar at Forbes Landing before taking a job at the local pulp mill.

Then, in January of 1956, out for a drive, he and Maxine saw a small house for sale right on the Campbell River.

"We backed up, turned in and bought it right there. I've been here ever since."

The move proved fortuitous. The shortage of school-teachers in the booming Campbell River area was so acute that Haig-Brown persuaded the school board to offer Egan more to teach than he could earn in the mill.

He took the job teaching biology and later designed Canada's first high school course in oceanography, which he taught until his 1986 retirement.

In the meantime Haig-Brown, today lionized by

Campbell River and the provincial government—parks, mountains and historic sites are named after him—was being marginalized and vilified in his own community for the strong stands he took on environmental and conservation issues.

"He wasn't thought of very highly by some people around here because of his opposition to flooding [the upper Campbell River]. The business faction did not look on Haig-Brown as a very welcome member of society.

"I remember attending a meeting after the province approved the flooding in Strathcona Park. Somebody, a lodge operator, announced, 'We sure beat that Haig-Brown.' That was the attitude. They were making big money off the boom. They thought flooding Strathcona Park was a victory. They thought they had won. That lodge is gone now. I've never forgotten that.

"Haig-Brown later said to me, 'You never win a conservation battle, but you've got to fight them.' I've never forgotten that either."

Then, suddenly as a winter freshet, Haig-Brown was gone himself, dead, his voice silent except for the legacy of twenty-eight eloquent and far-seeing books.

"I was one of the pallbearers at his funeral," Egan said. "It was one of most awful times, in a way. I found it so hard to believe that a man with a stature like that—a giant of our time—was dead. How could that be?"

Then the old fly fisherman showed me some of his treasures, maps drawn from memory long ago, hand sketched by Haig-Brown himself with directions to the best dry- and wet-fly water on Vancouver Island rivers, some so remote that few anglers fish them.

The two maps he showed me, with their deft, confident outlines of landmarks on the Nimpkish and Campbell rivers, revealed in a few detailed pen strokes the mind of a man who loved the land and remembered its forms and the way it is shaped and burnished by the life-giving waters we so casually exploit and abuse for short-term gain.

These maps of a vanished world—before the old growth was cut down, the rivers dammed, the watersheds mined, before the malls and the sewage outfalls—they too will be part of the public legacy of Roderick Haig-Brown and a gift to us from his friend Van Egan, thanks to the *Courier-Islander* and its sense of public duty in publishing the memoir that began as finger exercises.

When Winter's Light Fades

Every fall, for many years, I'd make the long drive to the meandering Tawatinaw River, south of Athabasca Landing in Northern Alberta, just to witness the tamaracks blazing like torches against the tight black nap of spruce that covers the hillsides. As the sharp days of autumn draw in, these strange deciduous conifers turn a throbbing, lustrous yellow before shedding their needles before the long winter sleep descends upon Canada's vast boreal forest from Labrador to the Tatshenshini.

Tamaracks, more properly western and the alpine larches, are distributed across BC from the Yukon border in the northwest to the Rocky Mountain passes in the southeast.

Yet if these heralds of impending winter deliver their message with audacious flair, there are subtler messages that the season of bounty is about to depart.

Out on the West Coast, all is sombre. Pale fingers of light pry at the edge of a dripping rain forest already deepening into the green gloom of early winter. Here the hiker's mossy landscape is now punctuated only by the luminous foliage of the salmonberry, its last vivid leaves still clinging defiantly to canes among the vine maple and wind-stripped alder. Already the snowberries gleam crisp and white among naked branches.

Meanwhile, in the high, folded country of the Rockies, travellers bound for the Pacific through the Crowsnest or Kicking Horse passes leave the vast arc of light that is the prairie sky behind them. They might have been lucky enough to hear the ringing sound of bighorn rams in rut, delivering blows at collision speeds exceeding a hundred kilometres per hour; the clash of their armoured helmets echoes off the tilted mountain wall with all the throaty resonance of a distant rifle shot.

Or at the southern tip of Vancouver Island you might find yourself walking—cautiously, given the violence of the equinoctial gales—along the huge granite blocks of Victoria's breakwater, hoping to spark yourself out of the seasonal blues with a glimpse of gaudy harlequin ducks among the dowdier seabirds massing for winter on the water. Naturalist James Luther Davis calls this the great Salish Sea, the shimmering confluence of Puget Sound and the straits of Georgia and Juan de Fuca.

Fall colours and the transformation of trees, the mysterious movements of animals, the darker currents of sex and human psychology: all these elements of the natural world are connected by one lambent reality, the length of the day.

Each second the sun pours 130 trillion horsepower of energy upon the face that the Earth turns toward the solar wind. Of this about 50 percent arrives in the form of visible light, our experience of it parsed into day and night by the rotation of the planet.

And this light, a presence we tend to think about mostly in aesthetic terms—a moonlit river, the flame of a last leaf, "the evening light that lingers on the wild duck's back," in the words of Japanese poet Ooka Hiroshi—is the source of all the teeming variants of life that surround us. It energizes the smallest creatures in the food chain. It drives the entire plant kingdom without which no animal life could survive. It regulates and governs the most primal processes of life, even human psychology, in ways we scarcely notice and barely begin to understand.

Who, except a few anthropologists, takes note that even in our high-tech civilization, the rhythms of reproduction and fertility still appear to be synchronized in some way with the seasonal variations in day length? Clearly there are factors other than light at work, yet conceptions in North America spike sharply upward around Christmas when the days are shortest.

And it's not just a result of lowered inhibitions during the festive season or the birth control forgotten in a fog of toddies, mulled wine and brandy-spiked eggnogs. In late fall, just as the days begin to shorten, the hormones most crucial to sexual arousal appear in elevated concentrations.

In late autumn we once again arrive at what biologists call the light switch, a biophysical phenomenon triggered by the amount of visible light in the environment. It signals plants and animals to prepare themselves for the arduous months that lie ahead, evoking patterns of behaviour so old they are coded right into our DNA.

Those animals and insects that can will abandon the bleak winter landscape and travel to warmer climes. Those that can't must either adapt the environment—beavers build insulated lodges and stock the underwater larder with leaves and branches—or become part of it. Some frogs freeze solid and revive when they thaw in the spring. Many small birds enter a state of torpor at night, inducing a kind of controlled hypothermia that decreases their heat loss and requires them to gather less food in an environment where it is scarce. Plants fall into dormancy. As long as the days are long, the trees continue to produce leaves. Shorten the day by a few minutes, and leaves are replaced by dormant buds.

All summer long, Peter Gerrard points out in his book *Nature Through the Seasons*, these leaves have been carrying out a vital task, "catching and bottling the sunlight." But when the sunlight falls below a certain level, this precious sap begins to flow back from the leaves into the twigs and branches. When you see a leaf that is golden at the fringes but green along the veins and stem, the sap has not yet drained. Once the sap has withdrawn, the tree rejects its own superfluous leaves, cutting them off with a layer of cork-like cells that both caulks and bandages the broken spot.

Photosynthesis ceases, and sap retreats into the root masses below ground where it will be protected from freezing temperatures until the days lengthen again, tripping the light switch. Then the sap begins to rise back to the buds where it will cause new leaves to unfurl.

In fall the whole process is accompanied by its own orchestra: the sounds of migratory birds gathering along ancient flight corridors that will funnel them south and spawning salmon splashing the river shallows.

On the ground, mammals like bears, squirrels and marmots begin to slow their metabolic processes, shutting down their large muscle activity and thereby reducing their internal heat budget. Their unborn babies already safely lodged in their wombs, they enter the sleep-like state called hibernation that will endure until the light switch trips again next spring.

The whole complicated story of the light switch begins in the heavens.

His famous three-starred belt shining in the December sky, his faithful hound Sirius trotting at his heels, Orion the Hunter is one harbinger of the change from summer to winter. Another signal is the arrival of the Rainy Sisters—the Pleiades to stargazers—a barely visible cluster in the constellation Taurus in which seven stars are visible to a sharp eye. Babylonians, Persians, Egyptians and Greeks all took note. The brightness of these faint starts in the black winter sky is a reminder of the dwindling light in our own world as we tilt irrevocably toward our farthest point from the life-giving sun.

On the south coast we will arrive there after darkness falls at a precise, mathematically predictable second on the astronomical calendar. The celestial appointment book is nothing if not exact.

Because few surfaces on this curved and crumpled continent are perpendicular to the incoming sleet of solar radiation, the light energy we receive is simple physics, a function of the angle by which the sun deviates from the vertical. It's another relationship that changes with mathematical precision as the Earth swings around its orbit.

Gerrard has likened the process that's triggered by the sun's apparent retreat southward to the act of turning the volume knob on a radio. Think of the radio as being at full volume when the knob points up and muted when the knob is turned to the horizontal. In northern latitudes it's this angle between the vertical and the horizontal that governs the volume of solar radiation falling upon the earth as light and heat. The closer the sun is to the horizon—the wider the angle from the vertical—the more diffuse and less intense the light and heat falling on the higher latitudes. The fewer the heat units, the shorter the exposure to daily sunlight and the slower the pace of plant growth until eventually the volume knob—the light switch—is turned off, triggering the vegetable kingdom's sudden dormancy.

So while the effects of this change can be abrupt and dramatic from our individual points of view—the sudden clamour of snow geese overhead, the purpling sides of dog salmon in the spawning channels, the brief flare of tamaracks against a dark hillside—in the bigger picture it is not a simple on–off mechanism, but a kind of environmental slider switch.

Technically we will still await winter on the West Coast when a thousand metres up the surrounding mountains, arctic conditions already prevail. And while Greater Vancouver waits for its shortest day, the full polar night has already descended on settlements in the Far North.

Those regions above 66.5 degrees of latitude—the Arctic Circle, that degree of latitude beyond which the sun fails to rise above the horizon for at least one day per year—are cloaked in an arc of darkness that curves from Old Crow in Yukon to Pangnirtung on Baffin Island.

Because of our 23.5-degree inclination from the vertical, the zone in which the sun never rises starts at the North Pole and expands southward as the planet moves toward the winter solstice, that orbital position on which the least sunlight reaches the northern hemisphere.

The rest of us notice this progression as a simple narrowing of days. Sunrise comes later, and sunset arrives earlier. And then, one day, those of us who work inside older buildings without light wells and picture windows discover that we can go for days on end without exposure to natural light. We leave for work before dawn to beat the morning gridlock, and having waited until after rush hour, return home in the dark.

Across Canada's northern shoulder the effects are more dramatic. Almost five million square kilometres of ocean is flash-frozen to a depth of two metres.

This has profound effects. First, the snow and ice reflect radiant energy back into space, reducing the usual exchanges of energy between ocean and atmosphere by a factor of one hundred, making the polar ice pack part of an important planetary thermostat. Second, the conversion of light to energy by microscopic creatures in the sea is interrupted when the thick ice shuts out what little sunshine is available.

Yet life is miraculous in its ability to adapt. As the light dwindles in the late summer, the Arctic char, a salmon-like migratory fish, begins to move out of the sea and into fresh water. The temperature of the ocean will become lower than the freezing point of its own body fluids, so the char must make its way to relatively warmer spring-fed lakes and rivers where it endures until the ice recedes and the light switch of spring sends it back to the sea.

Humans too, for all their godlike ability to control built environments through technology, remain linked to these primal rhythms in the same fashion as the char and the black-capped chickadee.

Twenty years ago a South African psychiatrist named Norman Rosenthal moved to New York to begin his psychiatric residency. He noticed a strong seasonal pattern in himself. As the days shortened toward winter solstice, he felt tired, depressed and overwhelmed by his work schedule.

But when the days lengthened in spring, he returned to his customary buoyant spirits.

Then he met Herb Kern, a research engineer who had identified the same pattern in himself. He too theorized that it was triggered by the seasonal reduction in sunlight.

Today, thanks to the research paper they published in 1984, forward-thinking architects design buildings to provide adequate light levels, and mental health professionals now understand that millions of people in North America, Europe and Asia also experience the effects of the light switches that are triggered in spring and fall. These individuals suffer collectively from what is known as seasonal affective disorder.

SAD is a light-triggered disruption that appears to cause the biological clock regulating hormone levels, sleep patterns and mood to run slowly in response to the diminished intensity of light. Recent research correlates the incidence of SAD in northern countries with the shortening of the winter day that occurs as one goes farther north.

In British Columbia, for example, the incidence of SAD is five hundred percent greater than it is in Florida. Move on to Alaska and the incidence doubles again. And researchers at the UBC's mood disorder clinic estimate that as many as 450,000 people from Winnipeg to Victoria suffer from seasonal affective disorder.

The symptoms mimic those of clinical depression: extreme fatigue and lack of energy, increased need for sleep, sleeping much more than usual, carbohydrate craving, increased appetite and weight gain.

Many patients improve dramatically when exposed to more light. Others benefit from the simple solution of walking around the block during their lunch hour. One group of Seattle researchers had success manipulating the room lights to simulate a summer dawn for sleepers.

And yet, for all our modern understanding of this primal dance in the timeless tides of light, perhaps we don't know a great deal more than the anonymous Japanese poet of nine hundred years ago who wrote, "When I look up and see moonlight filter through the trees I know that autumn, heart-exhausting autumn, is already here."

Speculations on the Stillness of Time

June Leahey tells me a story as we roll south from Campbell River on a deserted Island Highway, the American tourists having hauled their big boats, packed up the supersized pickups and RVs and left the road to locals once again.

The first September chill descends from the alpine meadows above Forbidden Plateau. Winter in a mountain province always arrives from above, not from a point on the compass. It sallies from its summer stronghold in the glaciers and snowfields of the high country, sliding down the watersheds toward the coastal plain that dreams into autumn under the illusion of Indian summer.

June doesn't like to drive the twisty old highway at night, even when traffic is slow, so my grimy truck provides an up-country limousine service to her old friends' anniversary dinner.

Offshore, outside the web of June's story, Mitlenatch Island gleams in the sun. The glaciated rocks hang eerily above the horizon in a luminous mirage. Science says this is due to simple refraction and the angle of late light across the Strait of Georgia. Physics aside, Mitlenatch claims its own place in legend as the Kwakwaka'wakw "island that never gets closer." Reaching back beyond the myths of the first comers, it is a presence from time out of mind, a measure of the vast scale of things. Against that gleaming rock, a favoured rookery for seabirds and sea lions, the longest human life seems a brief flicker.

June's story is about an American visitor. She got it, she tells me, from her bush pilot son-in-law, Bruce MacDonald, who flies float planes for Orca Air out of Port McNeill.

"Last Friday he took his Beaver into Port Hardy to pick up a charter. The fare was a tall, shy, soft-spoken man bound for a rendezvous with a yacht in Nimmo Bay. Once aloft, his chit-chat showed he had a detailed knowledge of the cockpit.

"Bruce wondered whether he was a pilot. The American seemed embarrassed. He said he did some flying. He was Commander Don Williams, whose last flight was piloting the space shuttle."

I think about this. A bush pilot whose main worry is fog and junk ceilings in those deep coastal fjords, and his high-tech passenger who lives the proof of Einstein's theory of relativity: at orbital speeds of close to twenty-eight thousand kilometres per hour, time passes more slowly and so astronauts return microseconds younger than the rest of us.

Once, inbound from Coppermine across the immense winter landscape of the Arctic barrens, I sat in a DC-3 cockpit with the pilot and gazed into the infinite polar night. A pale glimmer rippled across the snowy tundra; it was reflected light from a huge moon that hung like a bone-white medallion on the dark sky. Everything seemed motionless in a world where time had stopped.

On that trip Peter Sosnowski laughed from the pilot's seat. "Time is relative. Everything moves; everything is connected. The moon is hurtling past, all the stars are in motion, the earth spins under us." He tapped the gyrocompass. "That's set to a constant heading. As the planet spins under that fixed heading, we have to adjust our course—as much as twelve degrees for an hour of flying up in these latitudes. It's called precession."

Peter retired to a farm in Ontario, and I traded in my portable typewriter for a bureaucrat's desk. Years later I was recruiting a fashion editor from Montreal. Vivienne said, "You know my dad. Peter Sosnowski, the bush pilot."

Later I told his war story to June. Peter was a Polish RAF trainbuster. He'd take his P-51 Mustang fighter out at night and follow the German railway lines at treetop level, a deadly hunter of locomotives by moonlight. He was shot down twice. The first time he made it back from occupied France with nylons and perfume to impress a girl. He'd dated her once, but he remembered her.

Another former prisoner of war spilled the rest to me: Peter came back from the Nazi camps determined to be mustered-out in the dress uniform he left at the dry cleaner before that last mission years earlier.

The cleaner no longer had it, but he remembered a girl picking it up after Peter went missing. He found her address in the back files. Peter went to collect his uniform. It was the same girl. Things seemed auspicious. He proposed. She accepted.

June and I arrived at the surprise gathering of old

friends. There we heard Elsie Norman tell the story of her first meeting with Win Davey when they were just twelve-year-old girls in Vancouver more than sixty years before.

"She was running down the sidewalk. Her arm was broken and in a sling, and I asked why she was running. She said, 'Oh, shut up!'" It was the start of a friendship that lasted a whole lifetime.

That was the summer that Reverend Amos Mayse pitched his tent in the long-vanished forestry campground below the old bridge on the Oyster River, midway between Courtenay and Campbell River. In the estuary dunes and the waving seagrass, long since ploughed under to provide parking for American tourists in their motorhomes, his teenage son Bill met a pretty girl with her arm in a sling.

For Bill and Win, time stood still. If anything conquers time, love will. But the planet moved, as it always does, precessing under the heart's compass.

Perhaps, as theorists pushing at the limits of relativity now consider possible, all events truly occur at the same time: the distant island that floats in the sky and never comes closer, the still moon that races overhead, the place with the seagrass and the memory of it, a pretty girl with her arm in a sling, old friends, lost friends who are always young, a couple of teenagers finding reasons to walk by the river who wake up one morning to look back on fifty years of marriage, the future, the past, the story about it, the celebration.

The Last of the Blackberry Wine

The night I last saw Melda Buchanan, I'd been heading down Vancouver Island from way out on San Josef Bay where the breakers thundering up the white sand beach just south of Cape Scott have come non-stop from China.

It was one of those wicked evenings when the freezing rain can't make up its mind whether to become snow. Big, fat droplets splattered on the windshield with a granulated texture, then slid away into the darkness leaving syrupy tracks. The roads were slick with sleet and gusting spindrift. A cruel wind hissed out of the southeast, always a sign of nasty weather on the way, and my car rocked in its buffeting gusts.

It was late, and the street lights bobbed and swayed as I came down the long hill into Courtenay. I called Melda anyway, just to say hello as I usually did when I was passing through, and she invited me—insisted really—that I immediately come up to her neat little place in the apple orchard on the crumbling white bluffs above Cape Lazo near Comox.

Melda offered me tea, but when I got there, she decided I also needed to be fed—I did—and along with the cheese and bread she produced a bottle of wine.

Almost as dark as the sea beneath the bluffs, it still caught glints of light reflecting off the bevelled pattern on the glass into which she poured it. It would shimmer like sudden bits of flame in the depths, a bit like Melda's glance, which had a way of flashing suddenly, a reminder that there was always lightning gathering somewhere in the fierce intellect behind that cheerful smile.

It was her own vintage—made, she pointed out with great satisfaction, from *Rubus leucodermis*, better known to the less botanically inclined as blackcaps. The little wild raspberry-like fruit, native to the western side of the Coast Range, is dried and preserved in cakes for the winter by the Straits Salish and the Comox people.

As we sipped the wine and shared a heel of pungent blue cheese, Melda held forth on the bandits and rip-off artists who think they should be allowed to do anything to the environment as long as they can squeeze a buck from it.

I mostly listened, which was always a good idea with Melda. She was impressively well-informed and had a lot to say, almost all of it witty, passionate and worth hearing.

As usual she wanted to talk about the environmental issues that consumed her attention: the state of global ecosystems, the greed and stupidity of politicians prepared to betray British Columbia's environmental legacy and their own grandchildren's for dubious short-term economic gains, the trophy hunt for grizzly bears, government-approved incursions into provincial parks.

Melda's mind was one of those finely tuned instruments

that reminded me of a surgeon's scalpel. Fast, clean and able to cut to the bone of any discussion with uncanny skill, it usually held a deft one-liner in reserve to skewer the rebuttal.

No wonder she put the fear of God into the earnest blatherskites, perfumed purveyors of bulltweety and smooth bafflemongers who increasingly show up to tell you why this last remnant of forest would really benefit from a revolving restaurant with pink rotating elephants on top or that the park needs to be paved so that tour buses can stop and disgorge tourists by the hundreds at the newly franchised concession stands, never really considering why, once the park had been paved, there'd be any incentive to stop.

I guess their trepidation was not surprising considering the way she would deflate fatuous arguments with a logic that homed in like an Exocet missile.

Melda was a physicist and mathematician from an age when women weren't supposed to have the brains for those disciplines. She was born Armelda Anne McCulloch on February 12, 1924, in Drumheller, Alberta, and accompanied her parents to the Comox Valley as an eight-year-old.

From there she went on to Victoria College but soon moved on to UBC to pursue an honours degree in math and physics. Then she did what few women of her generation did, went off to graduate school at the University of Toronto.

On taking her masters in mathematics, she landed a job as the first female meteorological forecaster in Canada, stationed at Moncton, New Brunswick. She later quit to get married, eventually returning to teach higher math to a new generation of students at UBC.

Then she moved back to Comox in the turbulent 1960s, built her cottage on the bluffs and joined battle with the developers to defend her lovely valley from the relentless advance of the chainsaw and the paving machine.

Among her local accomplishments were the addition of forest lands to a park at Seal Bay, a curb on rapid development of northeastern Comox and the spirited defence that prevented further development in Strathcona Provincial Park.

She brought to all this her formidable sense of purpose. If she thought globally, she acted locally and to tremendous effect, blitzing newspaper editors and elected politicians with letters, organizing support groups, never losing sight of what the process was about.

"She's the only person I know who went down her drive and picked the earthworms off before letting you drive on it," her long-time comrade in arms Ruth Masters, then well into her eighties, told me with some amusement. "That's how intense her feelings for animals were. She was a founder of the SPCA here.

"Melda was a championship golfer," Ruth said. "She had a slew of trophies. But when she asked the course to stop putting harmful chemicals on the greens, and they wouldn't, she just quit. That was Melda.

"She was crusty, let's put it that way. She had no time for environmental destruction and she put the fear into a lot of people who tried to get away with it on her watch."

So when I learned that Melda had died suddenly at the age of eighty, I thought back to that last glass of blackcap wine with the old warrior, the way it caught the light and glinted with something else, memories of autumnal bounty, promise of the coming spring.

After her death many in the Comox Valley were distraught. They couldn't imagine how to fill the gap. But Melda could imagine it. She had faith. She would herself be the first to say, don't mourn, organize. She always knew with absolute certainty that in the big picture none of us is irreplaceable, but that one citizen committed to an ideal is always indispensible to democracy

What is important about Melda's life is not that it's over, sad as that might be for those left to fight the battles, but that she made such a big difference to her community simply by being true to her ideals while she was passing through.

Like that last lovely bottle of her blackcap wine, she was a gift to ease the weary traveller's late night passage through the sleet and the gathering darkness that she knew must precede every glorious sunrise.